Everything
I've
Learned
About
Motherhood

FROM MY
SINGLE-PARENT
DAD

Everything I've Learned About Motherhood

FROM MY SINGLE-PARENT DAD

Zeena Moolla

Thread

Published by Thread in 2021

An imprint of Storyfire Ltd.
Carmelite House
50 Victoria Embankment
London EC4Y 0DZ

www.thread-books.com

ISBN: 978-1-80019-421-2
eBook ISBN: 978-1-80019-422-9

For Pete, Zain, Yasmin and, of course, Papa. Without you all, there would be no 'fancy-pants' book.

CONTENTS

MEET MY DAD! (AND ME!)

'You know, Zeena, I raised THREE children
without any "fancy-pants" books!'

'You know, Zeena, I brought up three children by myself? And I was working *full-time*! I did ALL the shopping, cleaning, washing, ironing, driving, cooking – EVERYTHING! ALL. BY. MY. SELF. And, you know, for my lunch at work, EVERY DAY, I'd have a Cup a Soup and home-made cheese sandwich, sometimes banana sandwich – no "yuppie" lunch bought from a shop – just so I had enough money for all your "Maggie Thatcher" hairspray…'

I've heard this type of speech A LOT from my dad. It's usually around the point where he's in full Cup a Soup stride that I zone out or turn the telly up. This particular version of the monologue has been a favourite of his since I became a parent. It's usually said quite defensively, when I've asked that he adhere to some routine with the kids I've been attempting, or suggest that an ice cream right before their lunch is probably not the best idea. But every word of that monologue, and its many variations, is true.

Since I was eight, the middle kid of his three children, my dad has been a single parent and an *amazing* one at that. He's South African-Indian, of a Muslim background, and, as he's told me on many occasions, he arrived in the UK in 1957 unable to do much for himself. 'You know, Zeena, I couldn't even make a cup of tea!' he'll proudly tell me as he whips up his incredible prawn curry, yet to be surpassed by any other I've had.

I know it's too easy to herald single dads as heroes when far more women are raising children solo, without the same fanfare. But there's no denying, my dad, now eighty-three (he likes to remind me of his advancing years a lot, too), does defy a lot of cultural norms.

His own upbringing, one of fifteen siblings, was much stricter than my own (although my fourteen-year-old self probably wouldn't have agreed when I was sulkily heading home on a Friday night for a 9.30 p.m. curfew). His home life saw largely all domesticity assigned to women, while the men in his family were expected to bring home the roti.

'Your father does *all* the cooking?' one of my many aunties in South Africa would ask incredulously on every holiday there. 'He can make chana dahl? Really? He can't make chicken curry though? He can? Ooh, Al-laah! Your daddy is *good*.'

Their faces were agog in awe, and, I could see, some pity too. This life, especially for a man of his background, was unheard of. There was usually some female relative – a sister or cousin, maybe – to step in and help. Truth is though, even if we'd have had any family nearby to offer support, I'm not sure he would have accepted it. My dad has always been entirely his own person, fiercely independent and a natural nonconformist.

His childhood aversion to Madressa, the after-school Islamic classes Muslim children usually attend, exemplifies this perfectly. And the lengths he'd go to in order to avoid it still make me chuckle, even locking himself in the loo once to bunk off. According to one of my uncles, he kept saying to my grandfather, hammering on the door trying to get him out: 'I'm making wazu, Papa!' (Wazu being the Muslim cleansing ritual before prayer.) He was 'making wazu' for the duration of the Madressa class apparently and got a good bollocking when he eventually emerged.

His political views also stood out amid his family and, shaped very much by South Africa's apartheid, he was a big supporter of the ANC (African National Congress) at the time. While many in my dad's family found the ANC 'too militant' and 'atheist', my father was loud and proud with his views. He is a believer in equality for everyone and has rarely held back from calling out discrimination. Another uncle once told me, with huge affection, that he could personally testify to this after he'd referred to a man as a 'Mary', an excruciating euphemism for 'homosexual', and my father promptly tore a strip off him.

When he arrived in London to study law, aged twenty, after only knowing apartheid life in South Africa, he said he found the UK far more racist. While he, like every other 'non-white', didn't have the right to vote in his homeland, being coldly turned away by landladies and landlords with a simple gesture to a sign – 'No coloureds, No Irish, No dogs' – was, in my dad's words, deviously hostile. Immigrants were being actively encouraged to the country, only to face attitudes, abuse and signs, all without recrimination, that told them very clearly they were unwelcome.

'At least there was no pretence in South Africa – I experienced more racism to my face in "multicultural London" than I'd ever experienced in my whole life,' my dad huffs regularly and quite rightly.

His law studies didn't last long, and after meeting my mother in London, he soon dropped out, took an administrative job in the civil service and got married. True to his anarchist form, he rang up his mum and dad to let them know not to expect him back any time soon.

(I like to imagine that long-distance phone call as: 'Hello, Papa! I got married! So I'm staying in London now! OK? Hmm, what's that? Is she Muslim? No, Catholic. Oh, and I also dropped out of law school. Why are you shouting, Papa? Can't talk! Have to go now – I'm making wazu! Salaams, Papa! Byeee!' My dad assures me the phone call was nothing like that, and that my grandmother and grandfather were actually very supportive, but I prefer my version.)

In 1981, by then living in a small town just outside Bristol, my mum and dad divorced, and my dad faced bringing up his three kids – a teenager, an eight-year-old and a seven-year-old – completely alone. When I look back now as a mother of an eight-year-old and six-year-old, with a husband who shares the parental and home responsibilities, I can easily choke up at how hardworking and selfless my father was. His daily life largely entailed working full-time, cooking, cleaning up, checking we'd finished our homework, and, in the days before free school dinners, making our lunches for the next day. Weekends were filled with taking us swimming, outings to the nearby pebble beach, trips to the water theme park at Weston-super-Mare and taking my brother to his ice-hockey classes – among countless other kid-orientated activities. Plus, of course, washing our clothes, ironing our school uniforms, shopping – well, you know the monologue now. The most time he took for himself was watching the *Channel 4 News*, usually late at night, having recorded it earlier, and, if he had any energy left, reading the newspaper.

And while I openly eye-roll at the constant reminders of the Cup a Soup and home-made cheese-sometimes-banana sandwiches he lunched on as a cash-saving means, it's not an exaggeration. As he was still in the civil service on a mediocre salary, there wasn't a huge amount of money – but we wanted for nothing really. Because of the sacrifices he made. He forfeited any social life, any 'luxuries' for himself and yes, 'fancy-pants' lunches, entirely to prioritise us. And I'm afraid, yes, I did use a lot of hairspray (sorry about the ozone layer, by the way).

So, I'm telling you all this about my dad, as this book, while written from my perspective, with my experiences, very much has his influence everywhere. His massive-hearted parenting shaped who I am and, undoubtedly, the kind of mother I am. And while my own sense of humour, quite dark on occasion I concede, might not so obviously be attributed to an 83-year-old South African-Indian Muslim man, I can assure you, he's the biggest piss-taker I know. He knows how to turn any situation around with humour, and if that's not a vital skill in parenting, I don't know what is. But more on that in Chapter One.

So, having given you some background about my dad, I'd now like to introduce myself: I'm Zeena. I'm a mother of two, and when I first became a mum to my now eight-year-old boy, Zain, I truly believed I'd made a terrible mistake thinking I could be a mother. (Awful, isn't it, saying it out loud? But it's the truth and I believe this is something that should be embraced entirely here.)

My husband, Pete, and I had counted down the nine months prior with so much excitement. But when our baby arrived, and acid reflux drove us to dejectedly set up camp at my wonderful in-laws with Zain just three weeks old, I remember me and Pete admitting to each other (as we retired for another night of virtually no sleep) that we hadn't enjoyed a single minute of this parenting malarkey. It was a horribly sad moment.

If you're experiencing anything remotely like this, I want this book to reassure you throughout that you're not alone. I want to offer you friendship in book form, waiting at your bedside, breast-feeding station or on top of the loo roll, ready with a comforting and therapeutic laugh whenever you need it most. I also want this book to reassure you that life, as it did for Pete and me, won't just get better, it will be incredible.

Before we take our leave for Chapter One, I think it's worth clarifying a couple of points that could otherwise crop up in a disgruntled Amazon review (and while I'm fully braced for those anyway, I'd only have myself to blame if I didn't see off now the things I know might be cause for concern or offence).

First, I don't reference throughout exactly how my dad came to be the parent solely raising us, for the simple fact some things just aren't up for public consumption. I know in this age of living life online, lots of very personal matters are frequently divulged, and plenty with great intention, but that's just not who I am. Second, while I love being a mum and adore my children so much they spend most of their days being smothered in needy, noisy kisses, I also enjoy a cynical, frequently sweary laugh about motherhood (and while my dad is partial to a piss-take, my profanity is definitely not my father's influence – sorry, Pop). If this offends you, now is probably the time to inform you that this book might not be for you. Honestly, no hard feelings; we'll part amicably…

I take this hard line because I believe this: motherhood is not sacred. It's not a shrine a woman enters on giving birth and is expected to encounter like a maternal martyr in a vow of silence. A mother is a human being, with human reactions, and she is allowed to both love and loathe motherhood. She is allowed to laugh about it, and inappropriately if she so chooses. She is allowed to swear about it. And those who say otherwise can fuck right off.

I know I'm acting like a 'big lady', as my dad might say, using the F word and everything, but I want to be as frank as I can at this point so the tone and message throughout is abundantly clear from the outset. It is, after all, one of the reasons I wrote this book.

I also wrote this book to illustrate that loving, healthy families come in a multitude of types, which I believe my father exemplifies perfectly. And frankly, I was a bit fed up with seeing representations of any sort of diversity in the parenting sector sitting largely amid the serious 'specialised' titles, slightly ghettoised away from the mainstream. My dad's kind, wholehearted and hilarious parenting deserves far more than dry academic words and footnotes. He's not a set text! He's a real person whose existence, like many other woefully underrepresented lives, should be featured front and centre, taking up the space he so rightfully warrants.

I wanted to finish this introduction with something breathtakingly profound about just how much my dad, 'Papa' to his five cherished grandchildren, means to me. But nothing feels adequate. Some people are just too good for words. All I can say is, as human beings go, he is the best. And I couldn't have wished for a better example of parenting.

CHAPTER ONE

Laughing in the Face of the Shitstorm

'You know, Zeena, I am funny...'

Let me begin by congratulating you on your beautiful baby. Wow! That wrinkly ball of flesh, nestled in its Moses basket, clenching its fists like Malcolm X, is 'amazing', 'gorgeous', 'stunning', 'adorable', 'too cute'. Blah, blah, bloody blah. You know the drill. Your Facebook timeline is probably filled with similar since you posted your obligatory 'our baby's here!' photo. And that sentiment is both lovely and genuine – but let's focus on you for a moment.

So, with your precious bundle of joy here, you're most likely cherishing every minute, right? Basking under the gaze of your other half, clearly in awe of your lioness strength to thrust his offspring into the world? Or maybe you're breastfeeding in silent serenity like the Virgin Mary, or a woman in a Cow & Gate advert? Yes, those platitudes and myths are actual motherfuckers, aren't they?

Maybe it's not silent serenity you're currently experiencing, but rather a huge shitstorm? Perhaps you're ready to lob tubs of Sudocrem at the next person who bleats: 'They don't stay this little for long, you know...'? Maybe you're fighting the urge to incinerate the sea of magazine covers at WHSmith with photoshopped women holding babies aloft, smiling at their perfect procreation and their good fortune at not having knockers round their knees?

And perhaps you'd rather endure a nasty case of mastitis than face another awkward coffee morning in a community hall that whiffs of both cabbage and incontinence.

Look, there's no doubt about it – motherhood is amazing, and the devotion you encounter is staggeringly strong. But when you're in the eye of the shitstorm, veering between love and lunacy, wondering how this tiny, adorable human can wreak so much bedlam in your life, I believe you need a robust sense of humour to help save your sanity.

Humour has been a huge source of strength on many occasions throughout my life. But after having Zain, when the shitstorm clouded over our lives, I struggled to find much funny. Without a sense of humour, I really didn't feel like me. I felt helpless and hopeless. Was this it? Was I going to feel this flat, this humourless, about motherhood until Zain started sleeping through the night? Or until acid reflux buggered off? Or worse, until he started school?

The amazing midwifery team who regularly checked in on both Zain and me would sweetly and gently ask how I was feeling and, like them, I feared depression would stick its big, bleak beak into my life again as it did in my twenties. But I knew it wasn't like the depression I'd had in the past – it was entirely to do with the overwhelming circumstances I was faced with. It might sound trite, but what I genuinely needed most was a good, dry laugh to purge the dark days and give me some perspective over the shitstorm.

Without a doubt, humour is the first and best top tip for any new parent I can offer. I can honestly say that for me it turned things completely around, from wishing my precious maternity leave away, to relishing every last drop of it. And I have my dad to thank…

Papa is the funniest person I know. Obviously don't tell him I told you that. I'll never hear the end of it. But he is. He knows exactly how to use wit in the most testing and awkward of circumstances.

Let me give you a few examples:

- When Papa had not long moved to the UK from South Africa during the 1950s, someone (clearly having watched too many dodgy old cartoons of African people with bones through their noses) asked him, sincerely, if it was true that they boiled and ate people in his home continent. He laughed and smiled. And then said, 'Yes.'

- As a single parent working full-time, Papa's cooking comprised of many frozen ready meals. One evening after work, as he stopped off at the local Bejam to get that night's dinner, my friend's mum bumped into him and spied the less-than-nutritious contents of his basket. 'You can't feed your kids that!' she exclaimed. 'Where are the vitamins?' 'Oh, I don't know,' replied my dad thoughtfully. 'Have you tried Superdrug?'

- While he generally likes to laugh heartily at his own jokes, he can be the deadpan king when it suits him. A bloke once asked him where he was from and he replied nonchalantly, 'Bristol.' 'No, but where are you from originally?' enquired the bloke. 'Oh, I see,' said my pop in his distinctive South African-Indian accent. 'London.'

It's true, I've heard all these stories (and many, MANY more) a lot, but they say so much about Papa's super powers: his warmth, his emotional intelligence, but most of all, how he can use sharp humour to deflect and diffuse any given situation – even the casual racist kind. Each one of these frequently regaled stories influenced me, telling me to never underestimate the power of a cheeky piss-take.

So, as my maternity leave became gradually easier, just like everyone promised, and my heart could fill with aching happiness just looking at Zain, my sense of humour slowly returned. Comments that felt judgemental, rows with Pete at 3 a.m., energy-sapping sleepless nights, these were no longer pushing me to the brink of dark despair. These were now anecdotes to share with like-minded friends as we huddled like maternal comrades in coffee shops, cackling our cares away.

By the time I had our second – our now six-year-old daughter, Yasmin – and the newborn shit hit the fan once more, I didn't hang about. I was going to laugh in the face of all this *actual* insanity. However, cackling in coffee shops was now trickier, living somewhere new and, frankly, finding I generally couldn't be arsed with lumbering to cafés with a toddler and baby who screamed like an incessant fox on heat. So I decided instead to spew my rage on the internet in the form of a humorous mum blog.

With my daughter just four months old, and obviously her sleep behaviour permitting, I'd write at the kitchen table in the evenings, often with a delicious glass of wine – and it was immensely cathartic. Truly my father's daughter, taking the piss out of everything associated with parenting – myself included – kept me vaguely sane. I felt as if I had a little of my identity back and was robbing the shitstorm of some of its power. Turns out, motherhood just needed some mirth and Merlot (a nice, massively oversimplified, alliterative soundbite for you there).

I won't lie, my humour, particularly via my blog's social media, has often got me into trouble. Insane trolls aside, I've been accused of being 'ungrateful', 'a bitch', 'disloyal to the sisterhood' and even of alienating women without kids (which, given I'm a mum blogger, is a bit of a weird one when you think about it). But the most exasperating thing about all these is that they are accusations that would never be levelled at a bloke piss-taking in a similar way. How many male stand-up comedians with cutting and cursey observations about the shitstorm of fatherhood can say they've been heckled for their ingratitude, or lack of solidarity to other fathers and men who can't have children?

It really irks me because, make no mistake, levelling these sorts of allegations is just a means of putting a woman back in her box. And I include any charges of anti-feminism for ripping the piss out of other women in this too. Let's be clear here, we should always support all mums, whether it be about flexible working, the right to breastfeed publicly without vilification, or speaking out against the latest form of mum-shaming bandied about by gobshites on the internet. But frankly, supporting a fellow mum doesn't mean I necessarily want to sit next to her in the pub (especially if she's one of those Insta-twats partial to narcissism, #gifted clothes and peace signs against an urban backdrop). And it doesn't mean I'm any the less feminist because of it. (More on those Insta-twats later.)

So, if you're currently feeling overwhelmed as I was, perhaps wondering why you bothered coming off the pill and donning your special nightie in the first place, might I suggest you enlist the antidotal powers of humour to turn the shitstorm around?

Ten motherhood myths – busted!

1. You are worshipped like a sacred cow for giving birth

During your pregnancy, your other half might have sweetly brought you cups of tea and affectionately held your hair as you chundered like a drunk on *Binge Britain*, but rest assured, once the baby haze has gone, as you're likely discovering, things change… He can suddenly master an impression of a man in a coma while the baby screams incessantly at 3 a.m. – and that look of adoration he once had for you when you were glowing with child? That look rapidly dissolves to horror when you're angrily looming over him in a gaping maternity nightie, yielding said baby and an axe.

Some positive stuff to say: The truth is, yes, you'll call each other dickheads at 3 a.m., but by 6 a.m., you'll have forgotten all about the row, never mind apologised. Now that's true love.

2. Maternity leave is a lovely, long baby holiday

It takes a brave, moronic person to say this to a mum-to-be but sadly such knobs do exist. It's usually some bloke in Credit Control or IT who trills, 'Enjoy your baby holiday,' as you waddle out of the building clutching a bouquet and Baby Gap gift voucher. It's when you're scrubbing sick off the sofa, surrounded by full cups of cold tea, yet to brush your teeth at three thirty in the afternoon, that you remember what he said to you – and vow to bludgeon him to death with a bottle of Dettol…

Some positive stuff to say: As you're perhaps rapidly realising, maternity leave is about as much of a holiday as ten months in a boot camp led by a very demanding, volatile instructor. But – and you've probably heard it a million times already – that first smile, chuckle, word, step makes those yellowing teeth and cold cups of tea entirely worth it.

3. Boob = bond

Once that baby's out, it's like midwives and health visitors are on some sort of breastfeeding commission. Dare to mention to the more militant of maternity medic the possibility of formula-feeding your child before she or he can chew steak, and she'll look at you as if you've suggested making a nice pair of earrings from your baby's faeces. Of course, everyone knows 'breast is best', but when it's not possible for whatever reason to breastfeed, don't let family/members of the medical profession/the *Daily Mail* make you feel shit about it. Feel guilty, perhaps, for losing her in Zara while admiring a very pretty top, or deliberately breaking his toy tractor because it's louder than gunfire – but refuse to feel bad when you've done all you feasibly can for your child.

Some positive stuff to say: For the past nine months, sitting in your belly, that baby has only known you. So, whether you bottle or boob, the sound, smell, sight of you will instinctively soothe him or her. That's a mighty big bond.

4. Breastfeeding only hurts if you're rubbish at it

Again, this myth is all part of the big breastfeeding drive, designed to make women persevere, and keep the secret can of formula safely in the cupboard. It's true, there is the odd lucky woman who manages to escape any pain whatsoever from breastfeeding, but she's rarer than a baby who sleeps soundly for twelve hours. So, as you're getting used to your boobs feeling like throbbing lumps of molten lava, I suggest strategically placing tubes of lanolin, packets of ibuprofen and big bars of chocolate (to soothe feeling both ravenous and sorry for yourself) at each of your breastfeeding stations.

Some positive stuff to say: It has to be said that, yes, for lots of women breastfeeding hurts initially, but before you know it, it won't at all and you'll be looking forward to those feeds when you can watch uninterrupted episodes of *Keeping Up with the Kardashians*, and *Can't Pay? We'll Take it Away*.

5. You sleep when the baby sleeps

Everyone tells you, as soon as you're home from the hospital, to kip the minute she hits the Moses basket. It's sensible advice of course, and your body and mind are screaming at you to go to bed, but you soon realise that this is your only opportunity to eat, drink and talk about how shattered you are. So, despite the exhaustion, before you know it, you're boiling the kettle while writing a status update (to let everyone know you're very, very tired), and shoving some cold and questionable leftover chicken nuggets in your gob. Even when your baby finally makes the Holy Grail of sleeping through the night, you'll still struggle to sleep, frequently waking, wondering if he's OK or if you should stick a mirror under his nose to check he's breathing.

Some positive stuff to say: You will sleep. It might never again be the nourishing slumber you used to have, but you won't die, and, on some occasions, you'll even feel quite refreshed. Don't feel bad if you don't always sleep when you can – eating, drinking, worrying, moaning and Facebooking are all very vital too.

6. The woman across the road is a much better mum than you

This mythological creature might take the form of a neighbour, friend, relative, playground mum – invented by your mum, partner, mother-in-law but most likely yourself. She's up and out by 7.30 a.m. with all three of her beautiful kids, decked crisply in Baby Phat, skipping and laughing gaily at her heel. Her busy but breezy day will probably include gymkhana for Jocasta, baby craniology for Jack, expressive Bollywood dance for Matilda, and all before a live studio chat with *Woman's Hour* about how she became a 'mumpreneur' turning old socks into life-saving mattress supports for children with sleep apnoea. Man, she's a bitch.

Some positive stuff to say: Like the Wizard of Oz, pull back the curtain and she'll probably be a stress-head with mental hair, just like you. Plus, to make you feel really good about yourself, she'll probably have a set of in-laws saying exactly the same thing about you.

7. Only 'chavs' and 'slags' shout at their kids in public

You've probably seen some 'god awful' mother in an aisle at Asda screaming at her toddler, who is lying on the floor, thrashing like a fish out of water, also screaming. You've probably tutted (inaudibly, obviously, you haven't got a death wish), before scuttling off to the safety of the ethnic food aisle. Well, judge away because like it or not, this will be you. You, yes, you – reasonable, kind-hearted, loving parent that you are – will be driven at some point to shout at your child in public.

Some positive stuff to say: So what? Losing your rag at a tantrumming toddler does not make you Myra Hindley. It makes you human. An epic, morning-long meltdown because you cut his toast the wrong way could probably drive a Trappist monk to use the F word.

8. Facebook photos of kids are for provincial baby bores

You might have sworn in your childless days, while bouncing off the walls in some pub, that you'd never be the type to bang on about babies on social media – but don't (and it's not a dad joke) kid yourself. The first newborn pic of your alien-looking offspring in a bloodstained hat? It's going up. The blurry shot of your unsmiling tot with red-eye, and the top of his head missing? It's going up. Twenty-seven thousand shit photos of her screaming throughout her first birthday? All of them, going up. You will become the mum you slagged off, and you can bet there'll be a pub conversation somewhere all about your endless baby pics cluttering up newsfeeds and boring the tits off your Facebook friends – just the way you used to moan.

Some positive stuff to say: Facebook 'rules' or 'etiquette' exist in the digital strategy documents of big corporate brands, and in the heads of needy twelve-year-old girls. If it's legal, who cares, frankly, how you use your Facebook profile? If you want to smugly post pictures of your baby, do it. Think of it as a return for all those self-satisfied holiday and posed party photos you're jealously observing on your phone, while while slumped in front of *Emmerdale*, twitching nervously at the baby monitor.

9. Motherhood admits you to some sort of lovely 'mum club'

The thing about pregnancy is that women of all ages and backgrounds feel compelled to say something – and it's generally very nice. Other mums, in particular, smile, ask when you're due, offer up seats and wish you luck. But once the baby's born, it's a slightly different story. EVERYONE has 'suggestions' – again, particularly other mums – and often it's neither welcome nor helpful. Did you mean to leave the house without a hat on him? Did you know that her Babygro is a size too small? Are you planning to potty train him before he's doing his GCSEs? Take a deep breath. Smile. And then bellow: 'FUUUUCK THE FUCK OOOOFF!' It throws everyone.

Some positive stuff to say: You get increasingly discerning about who you want to spend your precious maternity time with and, consequently, you'll discover the mums whose company you genuinely enjoy. And they will keep you sane. The others, you'll scoff about in your first, sweary-mummy blog post.

10. You have instant maternal instinct

When they discharged you and the baby from hospital, were you a little alarmed to find your first feelings weren't of elation but more thoughts of: 'I wonder if pretending I don't speak English very well can get me out of this?' It's not surprising really, given the baby you've just met is a complete stranger to you. And when you discover that this stranger you've just birthed doesn't speak any English at all, well, it soon degenerates into a hugely unfunny, situation comedy as you flip frantically through *What to Expect When You're Expecting* and Google: 'How can another human being be SO BLOODY UNREASONABLE?'

Some positive stuff to say: Again, it's something you'll hear a lot, but every day really does get better and better. Some things will come naturally, and some stuff you'll learn. The fear that social services and the world's press will turn up on your doorstep because you're a terrible mother will subside. Because with every doubt about your parenting abilities, you should tell yourself it's a sign you give a shit – which makes you a truly excellent mother.

CHAPTER TWO

Why Do They Say, 'Sleeping Like a Baby'?

'You know, Zeena, all children sleep through eventually!'

You can't write a parenting book and not talk about sleep. Or rather, the lack of it. If you're one of those lucky parents with a baby who sleeps well, congratulations, you are very jammy indeed. And also, I must be honest, likely quite hated. But hey, who gives a shit? You get to *sleep*, so who are the real losers here?

For those of you currently not sleeping, my huge commiserations. It's truly shit. As a person who LOVES sleep, I found Zain's apparent aversion to it a real shock to the system.

'It's no surprise they use sleep deprivation as a form of torture in some countries, is it?' trilled a locum doctor as she handed over a prescription for some baby Gaviscon that she'd already informed me was unlikely to have any impact at all on Zain's acid reflux (apparently he needed to gain a lot more weight before he'd be permitted to have the stuff that would actually help him). Whether it was true about sleep deprivation being used as a form of torture, I'd no idea. All I knew was, I couldn't even muster the energy to politely laugh. I could have, though, probably found the strength to flip her off, given she'd effectively written the word 'placebo' on a bit of paper and nonchalantly handed it to me.

Anyway, putting aside the urge to flip her off, she was right. It was exactly like torture. My eyes were streaming with teary exhaustion, my body yearned to lie down in peaceful solitude and my head felt murky and slightly trippy. If Zain was the kidnapper and me the hostage, I was not holding up well. I'd have happily cleared out our life savings and remortgaged the house for a bit of decent kip.

However, I'd like to reassure you my urge to flip off various members of the medical profession (of which there were surprisingly many), and similar borderline-aggressive behaviour, was eventually placated as sleep slowly occurred for all of us. It's true, as I mentioned in Chapter One, it has never truly been the nourishing sleep of our pre-child days, but we're parents now; our memories and concentration will forever be depleted by those kip thieves. Because, you know, the thing is… erm… what was I saying…? (See what I did there?)

But no one likes a post-newborn smuggo when you're going through the longest, most excruciating jetlag of your life. So, if you're on the brink of lobbing shitty nappies at your other half's snoring head, I'd like to put my substantial sleepless experience to good use with these seven tips below in the hope of alleviating some of that fatigue-induced rage.

Seven top tips for surviving sleep deprivation

1. Embrace your cantankerous mood

First and foremost, waking with the demeanour of *Halloween*'s Michael Myers after a night of little to no sleep is not to be apologised for. True, your ominous aura is making birds outside take flight in fright as you descend the stairs, and yes, the cat apprehensively arches its back as you pass en route to the kitchen, but who cares? Trying to fight a pretty justifiable bad mood rarely does anyone any favours, least of all you. Instead, accept your glowering face, seethe openly at the cat and announce how you're feeling with an out and proud: 'I'm in a shit mood!' Then, a bit like Moses did with the Red Sea, let these words part people out of your way so you can make safe passage to the kettle, whereupon some salvation might be drawn…

2. Don't buy shit coffee

Step away from that own-brand, punier-than-piss coffee! You need the good shit. The kind that ought to be sold by the gram via a dealer. Because it's not just the wake-up hit you need – it's the indulgence of a hot caffeinated beverage that slips down like silk and gives you a beautiful buzz, not a hefty headache. Life will soon enough be filled with the crappy coffee handed to you at terrible soft plays and the many birthday parties your child will retrieve most of his or her childhood illnesses from. Frankly, the coffee you will be served then will be insult to actual injury. So now is not the time to scrimp. Get the good stuff and pump up a nice vein.

3. Clear Greggs of all the pastry

Calorie-counting, cutting carbs, crash dieting, any form of weight watching – unless otherwise instructed by a qualified member of the medical profession – should be forbidden when a woman has just had a baby. So if that eclair is looking at you from under the Perspex of the refrigerated section in Greggs, winking with a delicious, creamy smile – buy it! Think of that eclair as a little ray of hope, love and energy in choux-pastry form. Rest assured, there will be time enough, if you so choose, to peruse Boots' chilled cabinets for healthier choices when energy levels permit, but now is not that time. And let's be honest, on the back of a shitty, sleepless night, a snack pack of edamame beans does not pair as well with a brew.

4. Make peace with living in a shithole

Does the home you so carefully fashioned from earmarked pages of an IKEA catalogue and John Lewis swatches now look like Mothercare partied then spewed everywhere? Are there soggy, milky muslins strewn on the backs of chairs and across armrests? Do you have brown-streaked nappy bags filled with stinking faeces sitting on the living-room floor yet to make their way to the outside bin? Get used to this. Learn to adjust your eyes. See past the baby paraphernalia and bodily fluids taking over your once-quite-nice home. You need to pick your battles when you have a baby, and cleaning, my friend, ain't one of them.

5. Take all cooking OFF the menu

Hopefully visitors have had the good sense to rock up with food and wine on arrival to greet your new life. Your freezer and fridge should be groaning under the strain of casseroles and curries. To supplement these kind offerings, there should be a few microwavable meals nestling in between the gifted grub and a drawer full of takeaway menus – but this should be the extent of any mealtime preparation! Any cooking involving more than the piercing of a film lid and punching some numbers on a keypad is strictly to be the work of SOMEONE ELSE.

6. Master the joy of saying NO!

If you're not in the mood for visitors while you struggle to follow your own train of thought, let alone a conversation about what the traffic was like on the way over, don't do it. Being 'on form' for everyone is not a priority – the baby and YOU are the priority! So harness the power of the word 'no'. Great Aunt Miriam would love to drop by the day after you've given birth? NO! Mum suggests you start on those thank-you cards soon? NO! Cousin can't make his own cup of tea? FUCK OFF! And if this is a little confrontational for your tastes, get your partner/best friend/godparent/whoever to act as bouncer for you – the boorish, bald kind not adverse to a little 'roughing up' if Great Aunt Miriam doesn't get the message…

7. Accept help with a 'Yes fucking please'

After mastering the power of 'no', it's time to employ the services of 'yes please'. 'May I hold the baby for you while you shower?' YES PLEASE! 'Shall I make you some lunch?' YES PLEASE! 'Would you like me to babysit before he wakes again so you can go out for something to eat?' YES FUCKING PLEASE! I'M ALREADY APPLYING LIPSTICK AS I HEAD OUT THE DOOR!

People who offer to help a sleep-deprived new mother are frankly akin to deity. They deserve plaques, sacred effigies and maybe even bank holidays in their honour. And you'd be a fool to decline their support. OK, you might feel compelled to shower in thirty seconds flat, and fine, you'll likely blister your tongue inhaling that meal before the baby wakes again, but these are precious, often rare, opportunities to recharge and feel vaguely human again. Pride is not your friend here! Those kind, Nobel-worthy people are!

Pride did almost get the better of me when I returned home from that visit to the locum doctor, wordlessly handed Pete the useless prescription and then flopped in an armchair with my head in my hands, bawling like I, too, was a refluxing baby. Unable to get any sense out of me, Pete gently suggested that we should go and stay with his mum and dad for a bit to enlist some help. 'No!' I shouted between sobs. 'They'll think we can't cope!'

Pete sighed exhaustedly. 'But we can't?'

He was right of course. Zain's reflux was so bad he couldn't sleep lying down. We were taking shifts to hold him upright while he slept on us, and his feeds were so hideous he'd wrench on and off the boob screaming in discomfort. Every shred of energy was going into all of us simply existing. So Pete rang his mum and dad and soon after we were driving from Bristol to South Gloucestershire, where we stayed for four weeks until things started to ease.

To say my in-laws were amazing would be an understatement. There were unstressed showers, hot meals and someone else to hold the baby while Pete and I drank delicious cups of tea. But I'll always treasure one memory in particular during that first week there, when, after feeding Zain around midnight, I handed him to my mother-in-law who was kindly going to hold him upright downstairs, while I slept for what I was fully expecting to be about half an hour. Four whole hours later, my heavy, aching boobs woke me suddenly.

As I sleepily headed downstairs, I saw my mother-in-law sitting hunched in an armchair, with Zain nestled like a sleeping guinea pig under her chin, as she blearily tried to read a book over his teeny-tiny shoulder. I was so touched. She'd been cooking for us, washed and dried all of Zain's pukey clothes and now this. I know; I was one lucky mother. This was my first real stretch of sleep, and as my sweet mother-in-law exhaustedly climbed the stairs, denying it was any trouble, she explained that she just wanted to let both Zain and me get some decent slumber while Zain was happy to sleep on her.

I'll never forget how I felt the following day – like Wonder Woman after her tornado spin. I swear, one day, I will repay my mother-in-law for her kindness – money, jewels, a kidney, whatever she wants, it's hers.

Meanwhile, I could sense that Papa, almost fifteen years older than Pete's parents, while incredibly pleased I had the support of my in-laws, was also a little sad he couldn't do more to help. He'd been a very hands-on grandfather with all three of my nephews, but as I was the last of his three children to have kids, he was at a completely different stage of life. At the age of seventy-five, he was already slowing down a lot and had even started having his own naps in the afternoon.

'You can all stay here too, Zee,' he'd offered kindly during one of our phone calls. 'I'm not as young as I was with the other grandchildren, but I'm not *that* old!'

'Thank you, Pop, but we can't really,' I explained. 'Zain doesn't sleep, and the acid reflux can make him scream. It would be too stressful for you.'

'Well, babies are stressful, Zee.' Papa was gearing up for a cheeky tease. 'You know, Zeena, I did raise three children by myself – without any 'fancy-pants' books! I know some things about looking after babies. And colic isn't new!'

I let out a pointed sigh and reminded myself not to take the bait. My dad's retort, as if we were simply overreacting to a slightly possety, fussy baby, was something by now very familiar to us when we talked about Zain's acid reflux. It was as if acid reflux, along with the gluten-intolerant and dairy-free diets, was some new trendy fad that had made its way down from London to the West Country, and now all the middle-class wankers had kids with acid reflux. Yes, there's nothing like telling insanely sleep-deprived new parents it's all in their hipster heads.

Papa, of course, true to wind-up-merchant form, had no guile about him – he was only looking for a playful rise. So, like many of us around our parents, especially when they're lampooning our own neurotic childrearing, I rolled my eyes and changed the subject.

'Was I a good sleeper when I was a baby, Pop?'

'As a baby, yes! But when you were about nine, you started having bad dreams and in the middle of the night, you'd come and wake me for hugs! Sometimes I'd have you *and* your brother sleeping in the bed!'

This was the first time, now as a shattered parent myself, that I fully comprehended how enormously hard it must have been at times for my single father. I have a vague recollection of those nights. My brother and I would be snuggled soundly under my dad's big brown arm, encasing us like a mother hen's wing. The alarm would go off, we'd spring out of bed to get ready for school, while my poor dad wearily stumbled downstairs, ushering us to eat our Coco Pops as he hastily ate his marmalade on toast standing in the kitchen, bracing himself for a full day of work on broken sleep.

'God, Pop. How did you cope with three of us? I can barely cope with one. And it's quite a small one.'

'I just got on with it!' came his defiant reply.

I've heard him say this a lot whenever someone has admiringly asked him how he'd managed to work full-time and raise three kids. And it's true of course, he did 'just get on with it'. What else was he going to do? But it struck me as both funny and a bit heart-breaking that admitting it was a hard slog would be like conceding a weakness.

Afterwards, I mused on that 'I just got on with it' expression to Pete. 'Why do grandparents always seem to say it so accusingly? Like all other subsequent generations are somehow striking parents, forming picket lines and demanding better working conditions?'

Pete gave a weary, wry smile. 'You do have a tendency to over-think things sometimes, Zee – especially when you're knackered. People just forget how hard it was. Your dad's not casting aspersions on you and how difficult you're finding it! He's just remembering it differently.'

After I overthought Pete's observation that I overthink things, I couldn't deny there had been many occasions, especially over the newborn shitstorm, when his ears had been battered by the

offence I'd taken to someone's ill-judged remark. Below are some
examples of such stuff – some of it I *still* believe justified, but yes,
some of it the grievances of a woman in desperate need of sleep
and coherent thought, as you will clearly see…

- *'I'm so glad I gave birth naturally. I definitely think it helps
  you bond more with the baby.'* [Said by another mum on
  the maternity ward after I gave birth to Zain with the aid
  of an epidural, moments before I flooded the entire floor
  following my catheter removal. I like to think of it as a
  metaphor for pissing all over her stupid, smug theory.]
- *'Did you know his sleeper is sized 0–3 months?'* [Said about
  Zain just hours old, wearing a bodysuit three times too big
  for him. Admittedly he looked like Tom Hanks reverting
  to a kid in the movie *Big*.]
- *'He looks so much like his dad, doesn't he?'* [Said to me virtu-
  ally every day, by pretty much every fucker who laid eyes
  on Zain.]
- *'Did you go out last night?'* [Said to me as I was about to
  nurse my five-week-old newborn. I wanted to scream: 'OF
  COURSE I DIDN'T FUCKING GO OUT! I HAVE
  NO LIFE! I AM A SEVERELY SLEEP-DEFICIENT
  MILK MACHINE AND CHANGER OF SHITTY
  NAPPIES! WHAT DO YOU THINK I DID? TAKE
  IN A COUPLE OF SHOWS BEFORE HITTING
  LONDON'S TRENDY WEST END AND SNORTING
  MDMA OFF A POP STAR'S BACKSIDE?']

I did warn you I wasn't always of reasonable mind.

But while I knew my melted brain was often blowing things
out of proportion, I did also feel that sometimes people could be
just very thoughtless. So here is a handy inventory of things you
should always say to a sleep-deprived new mum (as opposed to

stuff you should NEVER say, if you want to spare a friend, partner or relative a ranty earbashing).

Eleven things you should always say to a sleep-deprived new mum

1. A new mum wants to hear: 'You really do suit the psychopathic, homeless look.'

When you pay a visit to a woman who's just had a baby, don't be alarmed if she answers the door looking fit to kill, with a piece of toast stuck to her left cheek, wearing a dressing gown that could feature in a Tracey Emin installation. First, she'll be very angry she's had to answer the door herself and second, she'll probably be so short of sleep and time that personal upkeep is generally limited to a wet-wipe wash. Just tell her she looks better than ever and don't mention that her unbrushed teeth are starting to resemble Baldrick's in *Blackadder*.

You must NEVER say: *'Did you know you have sick in your hair and a tit hanging out?'* The chances are she didn't, and you know what they say, ignorance is bliss. Like an unexploded landmine, leave her be. If you know what's good for you.

2. A new mum wants to hear: 'Apparently, celebs everywhere are having cosmetic surgery to get their breasts to emulate the cover of a National Geographic.'

It has to be said, pregnancy and breastfeeding will drain the life out of a pair of once perky baps, so it's hard not to stare at a nursing mum's boobs when they tend to flop heavily to her belly button. It's true she needs scaffolding not a bra – but the real support she'll need is from her fibbing friends and family, all telling her (especially when she stops feeding and they shrivel, rather aptly, like post-party balloons) her rack is just fine.

You must NEVER say: *'Did Sting ever manage to save your natural habitat?'*

3. A new mum wants to hear: 'You could definitely get your baby a big gazillion-pound modelling contract if you wanted to.'

A mother's love is, of course, massive but even she knows the baby acne and crusty cradle cap make her darling newborn look like a week-old pastry. So she'll always appreciate it when others take the time to pretend hers is the cutest baby they've ever laid eyes on, and make the effort to not obviously recoil at the prospect of holding her scaly offspring. And in truth, most babies are born a bit battered and bruised. Those people you see shuddering and shakily hunting for fags outside hospital automatic doors? They're not sick. They're the relatives of newborn babies, reeling from shock.

You must NEVER say: *'What is it?'*

4. A new mum wants to hear: 'I think it's great that you were so drugged up, you were off your melon for the birth.'

There's this weird, unspoken competitiveness among some mums that if they didn't have an epidural for their birth they should get some sort of Pride of Britain award. Birth stories are often swapped like tales of Nam veterans, with the blood, commotion and pain threshold escalating each time. How a woman chooses to give birth is of course up to her, but there's a lot to be said for being able to thumb a copy of *OK!* magazine while pushing a baby out of your vagina.

You must NEVER say: *'Epidural? Lazy bitch! Why not just get a general anaesthetic and Pickfords to do the job?'*

5. A new mum wants to hear: 'I went out last night and it was completely shit.'

No mum, new or otherwise, really enjoys hearing about the hugely enjoyable evening had by everyone but her, because she was at home attempting to cut her toenails in between retreating upstairs a zillion times. Tell her that you also went to bed at 9.30 p.m., after a fairly dull evening, with the only highlight being lots of people saying how much they were enjoying her endless stream of baby photos on Facebook. Should compensate a little for those uncut toenails…

   You must NEVER say: *'You missed a brilliant night last night. It's a shame you can't really go out any more…'* You smug twat. Yes you have a social life, but at least she'll have someone to check she's still breathing when she's fallen asleep with her mouth open in front of *Bargain Hunt*.

6. A new mum wants to hear: 'The Virgin Mary would be well jel of how serenely you handle that baby.'

When you see a new mum dangerously trying to fry bacon/drive a car/juggle knives while holding a baby, it's tempting, and obviously quite right, to suggest that she, maybe, perhaps, just-a-suggestion, shouldn't do that. BUT DON'T. She might explode violently in your face or break down in a flood of rasping tears. Instead, try a diversionary tactic such as wafting a Kit Kat Chunky under her nose and then lead her, like a dog with a chew toy, to a lovely, waiting cup of tea to drink with it. Then gently prise the baby out of her arms, observe while she devours that Kit Kat Chunky like a hungry feral animal and tell her you're amazed at what a natural she is with this motherhood lark.

You must NEVER say: *'I'm calling the police…'*

7. A new mum wants to hear: 'I can't believe she said that! What a cow!'

A knackered new mum will often take advice and suggestions, especially unsolicited, the wrong way, and will rant to her other half/sister/best friend for hours, sometimes days, about a misjudged remark. As the long-suffering listener, your job is to tut in all the right places and exclaim, on demand, 'She never?' You might also like to throw in the odd 'Fuck her' for good, authentic measure.

You must NEVER say: *'Are you sure that's what she meant?'* Yes of course, when The Woman Round The Corner asked how she was, The Woman Round The Corner was really inferring she was a terrible mother who deserved to die. What do you take her for? A tired, oversensitive, neurotic new mum?

8. A new mum wants to hear: 'You are a much better mum than me in every single way.'

Grandparents, aunties, uncles, friends, workmates, The Woman Round The Corner – with or without children of their own – all have ideas on the best way to raise a child. Aside from the stuff her addled brain will blow out of proportion, a first-time mum will undoubtedly encounter a lot of judgy questions: 'Why would you leave him to cry?'; 'You use a dummy?'; 'Do you really need seven baby monitors?' Once you've established her intention is to keep her child both alive and happy, it's time to park the passive-aggressive inquisition.

You must NEVER say: *'We didn't do that in my day, blah, blah, blah…'* In 'your day', kids rolled around the back seats of cars unbuckled, gulping in big plumes of second-hand fag smoke. 'Your day' was shit.

9. A new mum wants to hear: 'The baby looks like you, just you, no one else.'

Deep down, somewhere in our subconscious, our real reasons for breeding are not to keep the world populated with lovely, kind people, (yawn, yawn) – it's so we have our faces, in smaller, cuter, wide-eyed form, looking back at us of course. So when someone innocuously and casually observes how little a new baby resembles his mother, despite her feigned nonchalance, you can bet she's a little wounded. And if it's the hundredth time she's heard it, look closely to see her brow furrow slightly, eyes narrow a tad, and rest assured, just below those faintly pursed lips, she is suppressing angry language so blue, it would make Danny Dyer tut disapprovingly.

You must NEVER say: *'Blimey, you don't even look related!'* Brace yourself. A torrent of effing and jeffing is about to be unleashed in your face with the velocity of projectile vomit.

10. A new mum wants to hear: 'My word, I've never seen such a fresh-faced, youthful beauty.'

Make no mistake, there's nothing like childbirth and looking after a newborn to rapidly age a woman. As she bumbles about the house, forgetting why she's walked into a room and then remembers it's because she's just had a baby that needs feeding, she feels like she's aged about ten years over the course of a fortnight. Be mindful of this when you see her in those early weeks – back hunched, face withered like the dwarf in *Don't Look Now* and knees creaking as she lumbers awkwardly down the stairs to greet you. Suppress that gasp and instead, very quickly trot out this stock line: 'I can't believe you've just had a baby and look this good!' Her bloodshot eyes will crease with pride and her cat's bum mouth will unclench into a chuffed, gnarled smile.

You must NEVER say: *'Did you make the papers when you gave birth, Nana?'*

11. A new mum wants to hear: 'If and when you choose to have a second baby is absolutely and categorically none of my business.'

Somewhere between the six-month mark and the baby's first birthday, people start fishing to see if there are any plans for a second child. Why this would matter to other people exactly isn't clear, but it does apparently and a new mum who might be enjoying a bit more sleep of late, often finds herself batting away irritating 'baby two' questions. And if she's ever spied declining an alcoholic beverage, or within a mile radius of the ovulation kits and pregnancy tests in Boots, she is certainly, most definitely, without question, up the stick.

You must NEVER say: *'Hark! Is that the sound of your ovaries drying up? Chop, chop, time to put out again…'*

Seriously though, that last one? Can't a woman catch her breath and let the episiotomy stitches heal first? Jeez!

So, before we head to Chapter Three, seamlessly about parental judgement incidentally (I didn't just throw this shit together you know), I'd like to pass on some sage advice about sleep deprivation Papa gave to me, when he spied yet another sleep training book I'd desperately Amazon Primed at some ungodly hour:

'Why waste your money, Zee? You know, Zeena, all children sleep through eventually! Now give ME the cash!'

Brilliant! Sales of *The Contented Baby* and *The Baby Whisperer* are plummeting as we speak, thanks to Papa's wise words.

There's truth there though. Sleep will come: 5.30 a.m. might be the new 8.30 a.m. You might still have the odd night of gruesomely broken sleep. But you will sleep restoratively again, I promise. And you will be grateful and happier for it.

In the meantime, so what if you and your baby haven't found a routine yet? Babies have a tendency to (literally) shit all over plans, and speaking from the bitter experience of a parent who spent far too much time longing for a routine, I believe the sooner you make your peace with this, the better. If googling sleep training tips at 4 a.m., spunking cash on books and comparing yourself to less sleep-deprived parents is making you feel like a failure, don't do it! Instead, be kind to yourself. Remind yourself you're doing the best you can. Treat yourself to something that will make you happy in the here and now, be it a family-sized chocolate bar or the impractical shoes Facebook's algorithms are sneakily insisting you need to own. And remember – the fug of severe sleep deprivation will pass sooner than you think.

So put down the shitty nappy aimed at your partner's head, make yourself a decent coffee and tell Great Aunt Miriam to do one.

CHAPTER THREE

Parental Judgement is a Bag of Shite

'You know, Zeena, you need to be more like a demented moose.'

Imagine a new mum walking into a mother-and-baby group. As she looks around, she realises she's probably one of the oldest ones there. There are a few mums who are clearly already familiar with each other, and quite a few more like her, who have rocked up wary of making bleary eye contact. In between singing 'Down in the Jungle' and 'Five Little Speckled Frogs', she eavesdrops on another mum ranting to her friend about someone she knew who had just stopped breastfeeding. 'There was no good reason for it, other than she just wanted more sleep,' the mum huffs. 'That's just so selfish!'

Afterwards, the new mum decides to hang back for coffee with some of the other mums and starts up a conversation with a mother sitting by herself, looking as uncomfortable as she feels. They make small talk about their babies, swap stories about their births and conversation, as it inevitably does with new mums, turns to their respective, excruciating lack of sleep.

'I think at some stage I might try that "controlled crying",' the new mum shares.

The other mum is visibly aghast. 'I would NEVER do that!' she gasps. 'Seriously, it's psychotic!'

As the new mum heads home, pushing her baby through the neighbouring park packed with prams and pushchairs, she reflects on how the morning had felt like a university freshers' week with babies. *Except it was worse*, she thinks. *There were no Snake Bites and misjudged shags to take the edge off.* And as she chuckles to herself, she wishes there was someone else she could share that joke with.

By the time she gets back, breastfeeds and finally gets her baby to nap, she feels wearier and lonelier than she did before. She slumps on the sofa and cries. She cries because she's exhausted. She cries because she feels resentful, and she's ashamed of that. But most of all, she cries because she feels like she's joined a club she doesn't quite belong to.

It doesn't take Columbo to work out that that new mum was me. Zain was about six weeks old and while I loved him with my whole heart, this world motherhood had propelled me into felt shit. Making small talk with people where just motherhood was the common ground was not enough for me. I had a renewed sympathy for how my gay friends often felt when they were fixed up with people solely on the basis that they had homosexuality in common: 'Oh my God! *He* likes cock too – I'll hook you up…' (And yes, I've just realised I've compared babies to cock, but hopefully you see where I'm coming from.)

I knew these meet-ups were intended to be a help for new mums, and I could see for many it was a total lifeline. And I really wouldn't want to suggest they're not worthwhile going to – many friends of mine have in fact made lifelong mum mates over a latte and rocking out to a bit of 'The Animal Fair'. But I can't lie; for me, often these groups were more alienating than comforting. I found myself wishing we were all wearing badges as a shortcut to making suitable friendships, like a sort of non-sexual speed date: 'Not particularly defined by my parenting style – I just like wine'; 'Don't give a shit you gave birth without an epidural'; 'Not really into flat-Earth anti-vaxxers'… You get the gist.

Soon, however, thanks to a couple of colleagues also on maternity leave, a decent friend from an NHS class, and a few kind fix-ups from discerning mates, I started to forge some like-minded friendships. I began to realise, with massive relief, that I wasn't alone in my need for a dark belly laugh. As we swapped funny stories of judgy health visitors, unsolicited parenting advice from strangers in Superdrug and similar weird, shit encounters at mother-and-baby groups, I found myself wishing I'd met these women sooner. We were each voicing – with every 'oh-my-god, totally, YES!' – the others' thoughts, and it felt liberating. We openly admitted we felt less alone; less like shit mums for not taking it all so horribly seriously. I slowly felt more like myself, and before I knew it, I was actually enjoying maternity leave and celebrating life with my beautiful baby boy.

When I was on my second maternity leave with Yasmin, while I thankfully still had those sanity-saving women in my life, we were all at different stages of life and I found myself attempting coffee mornings and baby meet-ups once again. And again, amid the very nice mums I met and the fresh shitshow of coping with a newborn and toddler, I found myself encountering yet more 'mother superiors' who made me question why I'd bothered packing up a changing bag heavier than both my children put together and sweatily attempting to leave the house in the first place.

By the time I'd finished my maternity leave with Yasmin, I felt I had enough sanctimonious judgement to fill a book (well, a hefty chapter of a book anyway). The mum whose reaction to the words 'controlled crying' came close to a breakdown and the mother venting angrily about the 'selfish' friend who had the audacity to stop breastfeeding for a bit of extra kip turned out to be the tip of the iceberg. Below is a sample of some other, equally smug, exchanges. And I'm sure I don't have to tell you, I'm not making this shit up:

- *'A puree has never passed my baby's lips – baby-led weaning is so much better for a child's development, I think, than just mindlessly spoon-feeding mush to a baby.'* [Said in front of me to another mum, after she'd just produced her daughter's lunch in the form of an Ella's Kitchen pouch.]
- *'To be honest, he isn't really bothered about not being allowed sugary things like sweets or cake – he's always really happy with some dried fruit or a few slices of chorizo.'* [Said about a toddler staring hungrily and sadly at my mammoth piece of chocolate cake. And yes, she emphatically pronounced the 'th' in chorizo.]
- *'I know what you mean, I've got half a stone of baby weight that just won't budge.'* [Said to me after my own admission that I had three stone – by doctor's orders – to shift. And from a willowy woman, incidentally, whose baby was just four months old. And yes, I wanted to punch her in her fragile, beautifully bone-structured face.]
- *'Wow, what size are those nappies? Are those for your toddler? How old is he? Do you not want to potty train him yet? My son woke up one morning when he was eighteen months old and just told me he didn't want to wear his nappy anymore, and from then on, he just used the toilet.'* [Said to me as I was breastfeeding my twelve-week-old baby, with several packets of size-six nappies, fresh from an Aldi shop, sitting adjacent to my un-toilet-trained two-and-half-year-old probably happily shitting himself as we spoke...]

However, annoying as such superiority is, it's the passive-aggressive shaming that bugs me more; what I like to call 'drive-by judgement'. You might have experienced a little of it yourself? A remark or comment, perhaps seemingly innocuous, that left you with the vague feeling your parenting had just come under fire. Again, like many mums, I am very familiar with this...

- *'You're quite an overprotective mum, aren't you?'* [Said as I kept steering Zain, then two and legging it everywhere faster than Mo Farah, from running into the Bristol harbourside. Obviously a more relaxed, cooler mother would have been happy for her non-swimming toddler to plunge into murky, ice-cold, deep water, but I can't deny it, I'm just not very hip in potential deathly situations.]

- *'Won't she drink milk from a cup?'* [Said as then three-year-old Yasmin was drinking her milk from her Tommee Tippee First Cup. Along with potty-training and her sleep issues, I was fairly confident she wouldn't be wearing a nappy, still waking in the night for a 'cuggle' and drinking from her Tommee Tippee First Cup at the age of twenty-three, so I didn't really sweat it.]

- *'We don't own a television – it's just so mindless!'* [Said by a staunchly TV-hating dad, after I'd just said that the telly had rarely been off during both my maternity leaves. He was also an anti-vaxxer it later transpired and if I'd have known, I'd have stamped on his Birkenstocks.]

- *'Sleep is for the weak!'* [Said to me by another mum, like a shrill and officious headmistress, on the back of my complaint that I had barely slept the night before. Sleep is not for the weak, it's for the knackered. And people who bleat shit like this tend to be the same sort whose lips purse like a cat's arse around any discussion of sleep training.]

- *'Yes, my son had acid reflux too, but we just managed it without medication.'* [Said as Pete and I were recounting our miserable experience with the dreaded reflux. Pete and I grew very bored of constantly explaining that the acid reflux both Zain and Yasmin had was about more than just a bit of spit up and a slightly fussy baby. On this particular occasion, at the height of our acid-reflux hell with Zain, Pete shot back: 'Then it obviously wasn't the same as what we're going through.' I think Pete got a little under-the-sweater action that night.]

Obviously, these are just my experiences. Other mums have told me that they've encountered a similar level of judgement for things like breastfeeding a toddler, co-sleeping with their kids and favouring a Montessori approach to parenting. And maybe it was living in a particularly 'bohemian' bit of Bristol that gave a lot of my experiences a preachy, 'hemp-shoe' quality. But either way, ideas and theories around parenting from whatever perspective just seem to bring out the judgy knob in many, many people.

It only takes a quick peek at social media to verify the existence of such knobs. And often it's celeb mums the shameful shamers will lynch like bloodthirsty barbarians digitally stoning women in their plight for parental persecution.

When former Spice Girl Victoria Beckham posted a sweet photo to Instagram of her planting a kiss on her then five-year-old daughter's lips, troll twats went berserk calling her 'disgusting' and 'wrong'. When glamour model Katie Price shared a picture of her three-year-old son wearing a nappy while he played with his siblings, she faced horrible criticism for not yet potty-training him. And when Hollywood star Reece Witherspoon posted a photo of her toddler's teeny-tiny cinnamon-bun breakfast, she was slammed for feeding him 'too much sugar'.

Who can really tell what compels such unnecessary, unproductive and downright mean public floggings (apart from perhaps deriving some sort of medieval pleasure from it), but the message from those contemptuous camps is clear: to become parent is to become fair game (particularly if you are a parent with a vagina).

How a mother chooses to feed her child is probably where most encounter their earliest form of overshared, uninvited opinion. Both breastfeeding and bottle feeding seem to evoke equal angry judgement. NCT (National Childbirth Trust) groups, Mumsnet forums, midwives, health visitors, mums, dads, in-laws, friends – most new mums I spoke to in those early days of motherhood shared experiences of being quite forcefully told how they should feed their babies, often the complete opposite to their own preferences.

When I was pregnant with Zain, Pete and I had hoped to combine feed and plotted, like the plebs we were in our romantic pre-child days, to share the feeding. We dreamed I'd breastfeed during the day, perhaps amid a sun-dappled garden with blossom gently cascading around me and the infant suckling quietly at my perfectly swollen breast. Then as I'd retire to bed, our child in peaceful slumber in the crib adjacent to our bed, we planned Pete would swiftly assemble a bottle of formula for baby's one and only night-time waking, ready to sweep in to feed his gently rousing offspring, who'd have no problem whatsoever veering from tit to teat.

Of course, reality – being the dickhead it is – had other plans. Instead, I found myself saying 'fuck' a lot as the nipple-curling pain seared through my hot boobs, before the let-down kicked in. Zain would scream and squirm relentlessly in regurgitating misery. And of course, reflux, apparently aggravated by dairy and soya, shot our combined-feeding dreams to shit.

So, yes, like most naïve, new parents-to-be we were idiots. But it was apparent to us both very early on that it was the F word that seemed to cause the most offence when we touted our combined-feeding aspirations. The mere mention of formula would seem to fall into uncomfortable silence and pursed lips, particularly amid the bohemian Bristolians of my yoga and NHS classes. But then, as I went on to exclusively breastfeed both my kids for the best part of seven and eight months respectively, I discovered that wapping out a bap – you know, to provide *sustenance* for my child – could bring out the tit in people around me too. Allow me to elaborate with one particularly rattling experience…

*

As the nipple pain, acid reflux and expletives subsided, Zain and I grew much happier with the breastfeeding process and Zain could feed comfortably for hours at a time. So much so that I remember asking a 32-year-old visitor, who'd dropped by to welcome our new baby, if he'd mind if I didn't go upstairs to feed Zain but instead fed him on the comfy sofa where I was already seated.

His pale face flushed, then fell. 'Um, OK,' came the 32-year-old's awkward reply. 'But can you cover yourself up?'

I felt so awkward with his visible discomfort that I went upstairs anyway where Zain and I stayed thankfully for the duration of his visit. As I sat on the bed sweatily trapped under Zain and the cumbersome breastfeeding cushion, unable to reach the remote control for the upstairs telly, I couldn't work out who I was more cross with – him for being such a childish cretin, or me for asking him if he'd mind in the first place.

In the end, I didn't breastfeed Zain in front of people other than Pete much. Too often it felt as if I was taking some sort of stance, and to be honest, life was exhausting enough without constantly wrangling with a muslin to form some sort of veil between my hungry baby and the weirdos who sexualise breastfeeding.

When Yasmin was born, juggling life with a newborn and toddler meant there was less time to indulge such twattery, and I was far more inclined to feed wherever and whenever, instead of hurrying to some breastfeeding broom cupboard in a department store. I did, though, make an exception with the grandparents, knowing, and forgiving to be honest, that older generations can take longer to shake off ingrained mindsets. However, on one particularly exhausting day, with my dad over to help me out with the kids, I asked him if he'd mind if I didn't go upstairs to feed Yasmin.

My dad looked up suddenly from his newspaper and squinted through his magnified long-vision glasses in disbelief. 'You know,

Zeena, in South Africa, I used to see Zulu women breastfeeding on the side of the road on my way to school!' he scoffed irritably. 'Of course I don't mind!'

I couldn't get over how much I'd underestimated my then 77-year-old pop! With just a couple of sentences, before resuming his paper, he'd reminded me just how exceptional he is (and with it, eclipsed a 32-year-old man-child with his enlightenment). As I unbuckled Yasmin from her bouncer to feed her on the sofa, I kept glancing at him with renewed pride.

I've never had those 'mother–daughter' moments my friends would talk about with my dad. We never had the period chat. We never spoke about boyfriends. We never bra-shopped (as my horrified South African aunties can testify when they hurriedly bought eleven-year-old me a training bra, pretty much the day after we'd landed for a holiday and my budding boobs greeted them at Durban International). My father is honest and endearingly open, but he's always been undoubtedly reserved about 'such matters' – and that's a lot to do with culture. I never knew he was fine with me breastfeeding in front of him, because he'd never said so. He wouldn't. It's just not who he is.

'I'm not made that way, Zee,' he gently told me once when I was snottily accusing him in an angry row, fuelled by hormonal rage, of 'never understanding'. I don't actually recall what it was I was accusing him of not understanding, but I remember clearly the stark gear change when he'd said that to me. He'd suddenly gone from shouting angrily back at me to an exhausted tone, and I felt bad in spite of my teenage angst. My Indian-Muslim dad was reminding me of who he was and where he was from.

So, twenty-seven years later, watching him busying himself with the paper because he didn't want a conversation about breastfeeding, he just wanted me to know he wasn't some provincial moron, I honestly thought I could cry. My heart was overwhelmed with love for him and his way of showing me support. True, he's no

Oprah, but he can sometimes cut through bullshit with such little affectation that his sincerity means that much more.

He dished out more loving-but-awkward support again, when, after I'd had a particularly rough week of contending with a fussing baby and restless toddler, he'd driven over for his regular Friday visit to help me with Zain and Yasmin again. I was tired and tetchy, and when my dad pointed out the coffee I'd made for him wasn't sugared enough for his tastes, I snapped at him (even approaching fifty, I still often revert to a teenager with my dad). As I heard him self-pityingly mutter, 'Oh, shout at an old man why don't you?' I flounced to the kitchen, swearing under my breath, to spoon more sugar in his coffee. My dad followed me. 'What's wrong with you?' he barked. The question itself was like a match to my very short fuse.

'I don't sleep! I barely have enough time to even use the loo! I rarely leave the house unless it's to drive to Tesco! Zain still isn't potty trained! And I feel like I'm a bad mother!' My face had crumpled into a sob like Zain's did when he'd misplace his beloved stuffed elephant, or I'd had the audacity to present the wrong colour of spoon for his morning yoghurt.

'Don't be silly, Zee!' My dad was still shouting, but his brown eyes had softened and widened with both concern and the typical unease he had with this type of conversation. 'You know, Zeena, in South African-Indian families, all the women – mothers, grandmothers, in-laws, aunties, cousins – help a woman who's had a baby; you're doing all this without that! You're not bad, don't be silly! You're doing fine, Zee…'

He shifted awkwardly in front of me as I cried into his now over-sugared coffee cup. Blowing my nose into a piece of kitchen towel, I slowly regained composure. I was grateful to my dad for his attempt at empathy, however visibly he was regretting following me into the kitchen.

'Thanks, Dad,' I mumbled. 'But loads of mums are doing this without that sort of help and they seem to cope so much better than me. A mum I met at soft play has two kids the same age as Zain and Yasmin, and she does everything amazingly by herself while her husband is at work. Her toddler doesn't watch any telly or have any sugar; she did some hippy sleep training and now her baby sleeps all night; they're always out on nature trails or planting stuff on their allotment…'

'People lie, you know, Zee!' Papa interrupted, his face breaking into his trademark mischievous smile, a precursor to a Papa piss-take. 'And you know, Zeena, you are very oversensitive. Why must you think so much about what she says? Of all my three children, you were always worrying about what "someone said". "Da-deee! Someone said I'm smelling!"; "Da-deee! Someone said boo to me!"; "Da-deee! I'm crying!"'

I wanted to be annoyed, but I could hear myself chuckling at his impression of my crumpled, crying face.

'You know, Zeena' – I could tell my pop was now much happier and hitting his stride, having shaken off his disquiet around my meltdown – 'like I told you when you were small, you must just do this at people when they make you feel bad…' Papa poked out his tongue, stuck a thumb in each ear and flapped his fingers up and down. He looked like a demented moose.

This was advice he'd almost certainly never given to me, and I can assure you, I never stuck out my tongue and flapped my fingers out of my ears at people who made me feel bad. But it was Papa's inimitable style of defusing a situation with humour. And of course, in his weird and wonderful way, he was right. I was taking it all way too seriously. Papa didn't waste hours worrying about how much telly we consumed or the lack of nature trails we ventured on – there was no time! He was busy working full-time and keeping us alive and happy!

As a single parent of course, Papa was no stranger to judgement. And while it's generally mothers raising kids alone who

undoubtedly get the rawest deal when it comes to stale, stigmatised stereotypes, my pop did have his own encounters with the
parenting police.

I'd like to share a sample of such single-parent shaming Papa
contended with, emphasising that his experience was largely
the 'drive-by' kind; his gender – as Papa fully concedes himself
– likely spared him from the franker, recurrent attacks of being
'irresponsible', 'sponging' and 'promiscuous' generally reserved for
single mothers (and I'm quoting directly from the *Daily Mail*'s
'comments' section, *of course*).

'You can't feed your kids ready meals!'

I often found myself quite resentful at the teasing my dad sometimes received about his lack of home cooking. He could, as I've
mentioned, make gorgeous curry, but thanks to being consider-
ably time-poor and his curry-loathing kids (I know – the *shame* I
feel now), Papa had little choice but to keep things as quick and
simple as possible. The friend's mum I mentioned in Chapter One
who'd shamed my dad's basket contents in Bejam was one such
culprit. She'd also regaled me with the incident in which she'd
asked my dad where the vitamins were in his frozen ready-meal
choices; good-naturedly laughing at my dad's retort directing her
to Superdrug. But I was quietly cross with her. I knew his quick
wit would have masked how he was feeling. What parent wouldn't
feel judged by such comments? But for me, she'd been particularly
insensitive to my dad being a single parent.

Still now, I can feel riled when I hear or read some patronising
observation inferring poverty or single parenting is not sufficient
grounds for the absence of home-cooked family meals. Let's be
honest, most responsible for such condescension (largely TV chefs
and journalists), won't have a clue what it feels like to be (or see)

an exhausted single parent walking through the door after a long day at work, having to defuse some sibling spat, before summoning the energy to rustle up a family meal among the many parental chores that lie ahead of them that evening.

Of course, as my brother and I got older, Papa assigned housework responsibilities to us each, with my sister then at university. But there was still very little 'free time' for him. With my kids now six and eight, similar ages to me and my brother when Papa was raising us alone, I can grasp how relentless it must have felt for him at times. Pete and I have each other to lean on, and while I freely moan about Pete's own untidiness and tendency to tell me 27,000 times that he's put a wash on or emptied the bin (or some other household chore I regularly do without the fanfare), we do pretty much shoulder everything together.

On a typical post-school day, one of us will cook, while the other helps with the homework or plays a game. I might shower the kids and get them ready for bed, while Pete clears up the debris downstairs and prepares the next day's lunches and snacks. If both kids have an after-school club or a playdate, we can each do a pick-up. By the time the kids are in bed, we're exhausted admittedly, but there's usually enough time for an evening of telly with a brew or, for the days it's most called for, a glass of wine. Papa didn't have that support to lean on. His day generally didn't end until ten or eleven at night. He'd go to bed, just to repeat the whole thing again the following day. Some evenings I remember him yawning incessantly, his eyes streaming with fatigue as he tucked me in for bed, smothering my forehead in kisses.

So frankly, those microwavable lasagne meals and Findus crispy pancakes were not the work of the devil. They were the sustenance in our bellies that afforded my self-sacrificing, hardworking, devoted single-parent dad a little precious sanity.

'God, it must be a hard life for you all'

There's no denying that my dad had it tough; raising three children alone around a full-time job was no picnic. But that inference, that life must be a bit bleak, was totally inaccurate. And while this sort of remark was often said sympathetically, I sometimes sensed there was a certain amount of dejected projection – almost like, 'God, I wouldn't want *that* life' – because in their view, our single-parent family was somehow broken and sad. But we were far from it.

My childhood with Papa contains some of the happiest memories of my life, and actually, we never really wanted for anything. It's true, we didn't have a lot of money growing up and that might have meant the odd school trip had to be forfeited, or we would likely only get one or two of those toys on the optimistically earmarked pages of the Argos catalogue for Christmas (despite our best efforts). But there's nothing 'broken' about a family headed by a parent who does everything they feasibly can to provide a safe, happy environment. And (newsflash) some two-parent families, particularly when the relationship is deeply unhappy, can be far more dysfunctional and damaging. But I guess research into the effects of couples being together when they really shouldn't be doesn't make for great bigot-baiting headlines depicting a 'broken' Britain.

'How does a single dad understand a teenage daughter?'

Short answer? He doesn't. Because no parent, to my knowledge, 'understands' their teenage child! And certainly not from the teenage child's perspective. But while I can't genuinely say Papa and I were having heart-to-hearts while he blow-dried my hair – and certainly the mortifying curfews he set me and my siblings didn't really exemplify huge adolescent understanding – he did,

however, make a few concessions to our teenage rites of passage.
For instance, I was allowed to wear a little make-up when I was
thirteen (and kudos where it's deserved, it was my older sister who
did the groundwork here), while many of my friends weren't. And
when the latest 1980s fashion was doing the rounds, before I got
my Saturday job and bought my own clothes, Papa would do his
best where possible to accommodate my teenage trend-compliance
needs too.

When I was about fourteen, I'd set my heart on a pair of pixie
boots. I'd been nagging my dad about buying me a pair as 'everyone
else at school had them', explaining that this in itself put me at a
gross disadvantage of ever having the respect of my peers (although
I think the words I actually used were 'it's SO unfair'). Finally,
he relented and, as he did for most of our non-school uniform
clothes, took me to Eastville Market, a canvassed, hotchpotch
paradise of clothes, food and miscellaneous household items just
off the M32 in Bristol.

Papa loved that market in particular because of the mainly Asian
stallholders who would often indulge my pop in a little chit-chat,
once he'd established which South Asian dialect was their mother
tongue or second language (Papa is fairly conversational in several).
When I'd finally found the boots I simply had to have, my dad
picked them up from the stall, winced at the price and approached
the Asian seller. As I watched him attempt a few languages to
strike up a conversation with the increasingly irritable stallholder,
I started to wince with mortification. I was sure my dad, ever the
haggler, was going to have to admit defeat on this one and I was
about to go home pixie-bootless.

Finally, just as I was contemplating sidling over to a nearby
plastic homeware stall and pretending I wasn't with him, I saw
the stallholder's face crack a smile at my dad's final language
attempt – he spoke Urdu it turned out! Charmed, probably, by

Papa's persistence, he agreed a discount, I had my precious pixies and we went home with a celebratory samosa each.

OK, Papa wasn't exactly the teen whisperer, but his efforts, particularly considering his own much stricter background, were pretty exceptional. I even had a boyfriend in my teenage years for a while, and although Papa wasn't exactly thrilled about it, my South African female cousins, amazed at my dad's 'modern' parenting, had virtually keeled over when I'd told them I'd been allowed to date a boy. To them, he was as cool as Aamir Khan (the Bollywood star, not the boxer), in an upturned collar.

'You didn't want to send the kids to Madressa?'

This, posed more as an accusation than an actual question, was largely said to my pop by older family members in South Africa. Even I occasionally bore the brunt of such critical comments...

While in South Africa, visiting there alone aged about seventeen, I remember listening to an older auntie as she complained in Gujarati to another auntie that my father should have sent his three children to Madressa to learn about Islam. There were many of us sitting and eating lunch together, and although I don't speak the language, the Gujarati my family in South Africa speak is often spoken quite fragmentedly, mashed with English words. So, as I observed my fellow diners, my lovely aunties and cousins, busying themselves with passing the Khuri Kitchri and steadfastly not looking at me, I soon twigged she was saying something that concerned me, and I tried to tune in.

My poor auntie, visibly squirming on the receiving end of the very gesticulated speech, interrupted her just as the older auntie was hitting her stride: '*Na, ma,*' she scolded reverentially. '*Harchou joh, inner jaraa Gujarati humjar pareh.*' (Which in my family's Gujarati dialect, loosely means 'she understands a little Gujarati'.)

When I told that auntie afterwards that I'd followed the gist of what was said, she laughed and, touching my face gently with the sweet affection so typical of my South African family, added, 'She's just showing in her way she cares, *gori.*'

When I returned home after my holiday and told Papa what my older auntie had said, he, like my other auntie, gave a chuckle and said, 'She just wanted what she thought was best for you.' And then with a familiar glint, added, 'You should have said: "*Punchart khala*!"' (Which roughly translates to 'gossiping auntie'!)

Papa's own aversion to Madressa was probably a fairly good indication of his feelings towards religious education. Although he sent me to a Church of England junior school, he often enjoyed overtly scoffing when I'd say stuff like, 'Apparently, Daddy, Christians don't lie,' and, much to my big sister's very comical fake retching, 'Jesus loves everyone, Daddy!'

Ask him now and he'll tell you he's 'culturally Muslim' – very much in a similar way to how some of my Jewish friends have described their deep-rooted feelings towards their faith. And while I'm an atheist, I respect and totally get that. He's been a teetotaller all his life, has never eaten pork and celebrates Eid with South African-Indian friends in London every year. He's proud of his background and very defensive of it, as am I, as Islamophobia grows at a terrifying rate. But Papa has always considered religious belief to be the choice of the individual, and like the true Daddy Cool he is, that's pretty much how he raised us.

'Do they not miss having a mother around?'

This was something said to my dad a lot and I can't lie, it drove me inwardly mad. First, it often felt as if it was a means of fishing for personal information about us as a family, and as I've mentioned, some things are just private. But also, it felt as if my dad, this wonderful parent who was doing absolutely everything for us with all the strength he could muster, was being undermined.

I won't lie, I'm sure things at times would have been a lot easier with a mother figure around. Not just for us kids, but for Papa too. But it wasn't all like *Three Men and a Baby*, with my dad bumbling about, gurning and grimacing at this alien concept of childrearing. And while, OK, he never explained puberty to me or took me bra shopping because he was 'not made that way', his nurturing side (something this passing remark very clearly pertained to) was enormous.

Every childhood sickness, my dad would be constantly attentive, dishing out huge hugs and kisses with necessary medicine and temperature checks. Every nightmare I had, that big brown arm would envelop me, like my very own daddy-dreamcatcher, until I was asleep again. And every time he sees or speaks over the phone to me, my brother or sister, he'll tell us he loves us in some strange mathematical quantity (resulting always in the 500s) that only he understands.

'I love you 580 today, Zee!' he'll say when he's particularly pleased with me, for, perhaps, sourcing the very specific pureed ginger he'd been hunting for, or turning the volume up on his mobile phone after days of him thinking it was broken.

'Hmm, I love you 529 today, Zee,' he'll say when I've been 'too moody' for his liking, or squabbling with Pete (he'll *always* take Pete's side).

There's no doubt about it, single-parent families can face a lot of difficulties, and yes, it can be really hard for a single-parent dad, much like a single-parent mum, to become the sole provider of all a child's needs. But I can tell you first-hand, a happy family, whatever its make-up, is quite simply driven by love. And this has always been in overflowing abundance from Papa.

As you can probably tell, Papa, with typical indifferent manner and pertinent comic timing, rarely cared enough to dwell on any such shaming. It was largely me defensively irritated (well, I can be very sensitive you know). But it's hard not to take such judgemental remarks, however subtle, personally, when parenting by its very nature *is* personal.

I can still take things to heart, worrying that my parenting is being judged, or comparatively condemn myself (I believe this is what's commonly known as shitty mum guilt, and something that sets up camp in our lives from the minute we wee on that stick). And it's true, sometimes it *is* you and not them. On occasion, it will be you blowing stuff out of proportion and boxing shadows. But the thing is, while hormones, a severe lack of sleep and adapting to a stark change in life with a sudden loss of independence can all deplete stocks of reasonable and rational thinking, there's no doubt about it, people don't half come out with some shit when it comes to parenting.

However, Papa is right. Disparaging comments and unwelcome opinion – well intended or otherwise – again, really need laughing off as a means of finding perspective, or resentment will rob you of dwindling sanity. And who can be arsed with wasting all that precious time and energy?

So, I'd like to propose a toast with one of the many cold cups of coffee or tea I'm guessing you have dotted undrunk around the house: May it be just the gums of a hungry baby getting on your tits, and not judgy and/or interfering idiots spouting shit without invitation or qualification. May you surround yourself with the sort of mum mates who, like you, would never dream of purposefully demeaning someone else's well-intended, unharm-ful, loving parenting. May you be blessed on the days when your new-mum neuroses are perhaps making your version of events slightly questionable, with decent, indulgent folk who eff and jeff supportively in all the right places.

And if all else fails, remember, there's nothing like a demented moose impression to take the edge off a shit day.

Which type of mum on mat-leave are you?

Martyr Mum

She believes sacrificing sleep, night after night, for her 'helpless little one', similar to the way Christ sacrificed his life, is the measure of a good mum. She regularly posts in baby forums under the username 'Amelia's mummy' and loves to punctuate with a twee 'LOL' and smiley winky face. However, emojis soon turn to angry, frowny faces should anyone dare mention – whisper it – controlled crying…

Competitive Mum

She'll smugly tell you her children sailed through teething without so much as a whimper; were potty-trained at one; started walking in the womb… blah, fucking, blah. Don't be fooled. Only half of it will be true – her insecurities are as big as her huge, very expensive, double buggy. Liar liar, pull-up pants on fire.

Earth Mum

Perhaps the one most defined by her style of parenting, this mum hates routines for children, and also won't allow her child any TV or sugar. When you spy that lonely, awkward kid wearing the authentic Himalayan poncho in the corner of the playground – the one glumly licking home-made hummus off a Tupperware lid – you'll know he's hers.

Snooty Mum

This mum type will rant loudly, in crisp well-enunciated words, about the sort of parent who takes their child to McDonald's or uses Peppa Pig and a big bag of Mini Cheddars to babysit their kid. Expect to hear the words 'lazy', 'irresponsible' and, in especially scornful tones, 'chavvy'. At mother-and-baby groups, she's also prone to frequently checking her watch and jangling her car keys just to show this badly dressed rabble she's not planning on stopping long.

Gym Mum

Complain about the extra three or four stone of post-pregnancy weight you're lumbering around to this mum and she'll pinch a titchy bit of skin (without which she'd be dead frankly), before bemoaning the whole three or four pounds she's been trying to shift – and her baby is already FOUR WEEKS OLD! Try to resist the urge to punch her in the face because then everyone will really know you're just a jealous, fat cow.

Girl-Next-Door Mum

This mother is probably one of the youngest mums in the group and, while nice enough, is a bit dull frankly. Very provincial, she'll sweetly tell you a long and boring story about how she and her best friend gave birth within days of each other, which apparently is just 'so funny' because they've always done everything together. She's also a huge cat lover and nauseatingly refers to her beloved moggy as her 'fur baby'. Refrain from making a crude 'muff' joke here. It won't be appreciated.

Midlife Mum

Likely to be the more mature mother of the group, this mum-type is so visibly stressed, she looks almost savage. Dare to speak to her as she attempts to bundle a toddler and baby into the car and you're likely to get shot a look that makes you feel as if you've just defecated on her doorstep. She's easy to spot at mother-and-baby groups, as she's usually the one with the feral hair, last night's red wine all over her elasticated jeans and pendulous breasts thanks to a very ill-fitting maternity bra she hasn't had time to replace. Why? Because she's very, VERY busy, OK?

(Yeah, that last one was totally me.)

CHAPTER FOUR

Oh, How I Want to be Free, Baby!

'You know, Zeena, it's not a bad life!'

'I remember seeing Lenny Henry in those Premier Inn adverts, where he'd fall backwards, while wearing a fluffy terry-towelling robe, onto a big double bed and thinking, "You LUCKY bastard". He could stare at the ceiling in silence! He could have a bath! And pee! And order room service! But most of all, he was alone! I never knew how much I'd miss solitude.' (Helen E, mum of one)

'Oh God, personal space was probably one of the things I missed most as a new mum. There's no preparing for another human being just being in your face pretty much all the time – even when you shower – it's so intense!' (Lucy, mum of two)

'I like driving, but post-baby, going from A to B, even for the shortest of journeys, was a sudden pain in the arse. I'd set off, confident everything was all sorted, and then I'd have to pull over and whack out a boob for feeding. Or, as occurred with each one of my kids, stop and change a baby entirely covered in shit! There's nothing like being stuck in actual shitty traffic.' (Helen F, mum of three)

'I remember a nurse in the hospital saying to me: "And what's the name?" So I replied, "Nikki." After some confusion ensued,

I realised she was asking me what my baby's name was – and my name was actually of no consequence. I was simply "Esme's mum" – and this was the way it was to be thereafter! RIP identity!'
(Nikki, mum of two)

The women quoted above – Helen E, Lucy, Helen F and Nikki – are all friends of mine. All of them love being mums, are very excellent at it and couldn't worship their respective children any more. But when I asked them if there was anything unexpected they'd particularly mourned from their pre-baby days when they became first-time mums, they didn't hesitate with answers. Because they're not Stepford Mums. These women know the truth will set you free – and if you're lucky, make you laugh (I still can't see Lenny Henry on telly without thinking, 'You LUCKY bastard'). These are the women to seek out.

I remember, too, how overwhelming it felt yearning for everyday things beyond the predictable sleep absence. I envied people waiting at bus stops, ahead of them a journey with nothing more taxing than staring mindlessly out of the window, pressing the bell and disembarking at their stop. I longed for every film, no matter how shit, advertised on telly that I didn't have the time to watch, let alone view in an actual cinema. I wanted to walk spontaneously out of my front door, without a ginormous bag packed with the entire contents of my home. I missed my pretty unremarkable life.

Certainly, I'd braced myself for forfeiting sleep and energy when I became a mum, but I never knew how much I'd miss, when I needed to buy milk, for example, slipping on my shoes, picking up my tiny handbag, opening the front door and walking through it to head to Tesco Metro for a pint of semi-skimmed!

Retrospectively, with this freedom now robbed from me, I wished that I hadn't been so casual and hasty about the entire milk-buying process. I should have bought myself a Kit Kat Chunky and copy of *Grazia* too, taken the scenic route home instead, even stopped off in the local for a glass of red and a packet of cheese and onion. All that time I wasted, narkily huffing because I'd run out of milk and had to do some actual walking to the corner shop! What an ungrateful brat I was! Why couldn't I see how lucky I was to have that liberty? Like youth and the young, freedom was so wasted on the free like me!

As I'd sit on the sofa with my baby clamped to a boob, while eating a hastily made crappy lunch one-handed and watching the free world play on through the living-room window, recollecting humdrum activities now took on a rose-tinted glow of nostalgia. Because these were no longer humdrum activities, they were hazy, happy memories. Subsequently, my fantasy 'day off' from motherhood didn't entail pubbing or clubbing or even holidaying on some exotic, white sandy beach. It was a far more ordinary day that I yearned for…

Eight gift ideas way more meaningful than bath salts to give a mum

Want to show a mum some love? Well, step away from that last-in-the-bucket bouquet and hastily bought box of Black Magic. To show her you TRULY care, give her back a little of the simple luxuries she enjoyed pre-kids, and, best of all, it doesn't cost much money at all. It's true, the best things in life are free – except drugs; they're quite expensive – so here are eight (almost free) gift ideas guaranteed to be met with gratitude by the old girl…

1. A mammoth lie-in

We're not talking some piddly, pathetic thirty minutes of extra kip here (meaning she's still up before Naga Munchetty on *BBC Breakfast*); we're proposing the sleep-like-a-teen kind of comatose slumber. Let Mum roll out of bed at noon, grunt as she troughs a bowl of Cheerios and when she slumps back to her pit and the smell of reefer wafts down the stairs, you can trust her day is off to a *flying* start.

2. The remote control

When she emerges later, treading heavily on empty packets of Monster Munch, Mum will probably be in the mood for some TV. Today there will be no CBeebies or anything involving a pitch, track, court or Gabby Logan. Once the zombied channel-hopping subsides, she will most likely settle on the sort of trash that requires little or no exertion – we're talking *Keeping Up with the Kardashians*, *Dinner Date*, *Come Dine with Me* and pretty much anything that involves competitive cooking in a cul-de-sac. Satisfied she is happy and not likely to choke on her own vomit, everyone may now wordlessly leave the room.

3. A poo in peace

When you're a mother of small children, a trip to the lavatory is rarely alone and, if it is, your backside has barely touched the toilet seat before a pair of pudgy hands are hammering on the door demanding the retrieval of a toy from a grabby baby sister. So when Mum eventually moves from her very comfortable, catatonic position in front of the telly to attend to the call of nature, allow her, on her day of worship, a leisurely pee or poo in complete solitude and silence. And if she feels the need to let rip a fart that resounds loudly around the toilet bowl, NO ONE IS TO JUDGE OR LAUGH.

4. A long, leg-shaving shower

Next on the agenda is a lovely, unhurried hot shower. Today, she will not be using the lather of her shampoo to hastily wash the rest of her bits. She will cleanse her hair twice, condition, exfoliate and shave the unsightly forestry growing where it is not wanted. Yes, those hairy legs have served very well as contraceptive, but after a horribly embarrassing experience involving a dressing-gown malfunction which left both her and the postman scarred for life, it's time to de-fuzz. It might take several shaves – and a Flymo even – before all that hair is gone, so give her a good hour.

5. Hot UNINTERRUPTED meals, cooked by someone else, served to her FIRST

So what if her idea of cooking is violently stabbing a film lid and resentfully opening a can of beans? She's still the main provider of stuff vaguely edible and deserves a day off from slaving over a hot microwave. Let her dine without cutting anyone else's food, hiding vegetables inside chips or bobbing up and down for the correct colour of toddler spoon. In fact, no one is to touch their own food until she has finished and signalled her last mouthful of fish fingers, chips and beans with a gentle dab at each corner of her mouth with a piece of (unused) kitchen towel.

6. Adult conversation all about HER

After letting her digest her fish-finger supper, invite Mum to retire to the living room. Then, as she reclines like a less graceful, more cumbersome Botticelli on the sofa, indulge her in some adult conversation. Not the saucy kind – the sort of intelligent repartee that doesn't involve impressions of elephants or a billion questions ('Why is that tree there?'; 'But who put that tree there?'; 'What man put that tree there?'). Laugh heartily at her jokes, ask insightful questions and listen attentively when she wistfully regales you, for the seventeenth time, with the story about how she once got off with someone who was quite famous in the late 1990s.

7. A vat of wine and a straw

With her earlier buzz gone, Mum will now need a new high. Empty several bottles of wine (the good stuff – none of your cheap plonk) in a big pot and hand her a straw. Stick on a rom com – something about a career woman who moves to a rural town, upsets the locals with her big-city fancy ways, before falling in love with one of them who she previously hated. Now look at her knackered, little face – she really does believe Reese Witherspoon is her…

8. Artwork with bits of pasta/tissue paper/bog roll glued on

Get ready to barf – here comes the sort of schmaltz that keeps Richard Curtis in business. You can keep your mind-altering drugs and booze, because there is no high like a small chunky fist proudly brandishing some home-made artwork with 'Mummy' in scrawly, forced letters. When it's time to scoop Mum back up to bed, red wine splattered all over her greying nightie and the credits rolling to *She Was All That and Now She's Not*, you will see clutched tightly in her own chunky fist, a cherished scrap of coloured card with uncooked macaroni and stuff fished out of the recycling stuck to it. This will always be *way* more meaningful than bath salts.

Over eight years of being a mum under my vast belt and this is STILL my fantasy day off from motherhood. I should've lived every day like this pre-kids…

Where's a DeLorean time machine when you need one?

Do you recall those child-free, heavily pregnant days? Did you find the constant need to pee infuriating? Perhaps complaining to your partner or co-workers about how disruptive it was to your day, relentlessly factoring in wee stops? Maybe you missed seeing your feet and foof, frequently whining: 'Oh my GOD I feel like a whale! I'm so SICK of it!' What about the fatigue? Did you turn in at 9 p.m. most nights, declaring you'd never felt so knackered?

How much now do you want to go back in time and slap yourself silly?

Yeah, I'd have bitch-slapped myself if I could've done…

Dear Heavily Pregnant Me,

It's me (or rather you – these retrospective letters to oneself are all very confusing), writing from your future. I'm Knackered Mum-of-Two Me. I'm here to offer you some advice. Not the shitty unsolicited kind from people with far too much to say for themselves. I'm here, like a sort of sweary Dickensian spectre, to tell you to come the fuck on…

So you took to Facebook to write a sad little post about your 5.30 a.m. wake-up call? The baby (I'd just like to take a moment to congratulate you on never being the sort of twee twat who refers to their foetus as 'bubs' or 'bump') decided to boot you repeatedly in the bladder forcing you to flee for a wee before you pissed the bed? And poor you, forced to drink tea on the sofa in front of breakfast telly while you slowly shook off your sleepy little head. Yes, it's all very annoying – but frankly… DIDDUMS!

That 5.30 a.m. wake-up call will feel like a lie-in! That wee will feel leisurely! And having that time to watch television, curled up on the sofa with a hot cup of tea, will feel like a frigging luxury! YOU HAVE NO IDEA, YOU FOOL!

I'm sorry if I sound a little harsh, Heavily Pregnant Me. And it's true nothing can prepare you for the beautiful shitstorm of the first year of new motherhood. But you know, what with me being you and everything, I can tell you there are a few things worth savouring now, before your firstborn enters your life and independence is just something you sing about (badly) when you're pretending to be Beyoncé in the kitchen.

Here are some of those things I'd like you to start appreciating in full, now…

Eat the entire confectionary contents of a corner shop
As you know (and have fully exploited), it is perfectly acceptable while you're pregnant to dive headfirst into a vat of ice cream having already consumed twenty-seven Mars Bars. So now, with your due date looming, this is your chance to cram in as much gorging as possible without any judgement or self-loathing. True, you will have a little grace period after the baby's born when energy levels are low and you can justifiably trough to your heart's content in the name of looking after your own, and the baby's, interests. But once that baby's sleeping longer, I have to warn you, filling your shopping trolley with chocolate like a contestant on *Supermarket Sweep* isn't so endearing to the average bystander. You are no longer a lovely, glowing 'woman with child' – you're just a greedy fucker on course for borderline type 2 diabetes. So hit that confectionary stand at McColl's now – and hit it hard!

Watch loads of films, even shit ones
I'd like you to take a moment and recollect that truly dire rom com you saw many years ago in the cinema with a friend. I don't remember its name, but even by your standards, it was pretty cheese-ball. I think it starred Katherine Heigl, who was a career-driven single-woman-in-the-media. She and some misogynistic guy hated each other but actually secretly fancied each other. Then lots of 'hilarity' ensued as they pretended, quite badly, that they didn't want to bump nasties.

Anyway, do you recall shifting uncomfortably in your seat, wincing at its terrible dialogue and excruciating acting, before you and your mate walked out halfway through, telling yourselves you had better things to do with your time? Well, hard as it is to believe, that god-awful film, post-baby, will be filled with nostalgic, hankering, carefree memories. You'll find yourself at 2.30 a.m. wishing you stayed at least until the inevitable shag, break-up, then an airport-dash make-up – because watching whole films on a whim really ain't happening for a while. So, do yourself a favour, select 'Movies' on Netflix and watch anything and everything, even the crap with Adam Sandler in (except perhaps anything resembling *Little Nicky* because that pile of steaming turd is just an insult to Harvey Keitel's career – apart from those Direct Line ads, of course…)

Get a completely useless, expensive beauty treatment
Now, as someone who can't leave the house without eyeliner and mascara and has spent approximately the equivalent of the UK's national debt on hair care, I am about to share some devastating news with you. How do I break this to you? OK, brace yourself: you and your current beauty routine are about to abruptly part company and you will often spend the duration of those newborn days looking like an angry, quite dangerous, sleep-deprived primate. To be franker still, on the days as a new mum you have time to brush your teeth and run a wet wipe under your pits, you will be winning (I did warn you to brace yourself). But here's the good news: you won't care. As priorities and perspectives drastically change, you'll barely notice the zoned-out Meatloaf staring back at you in the mirror – and not just because there'll be no time! But because when you're raising an iddy-biddy human, winged eyeliner and a tidy foof really, really don't matter.

So, while you can still lumber up the high street, now is the time to book yourself a luxurious, pregnant-friendly, utterly unnecessary treatment. And sure, if you can be faffed (or rather foofed), get your bikini line seen to too, because that thing will need a landscape gardener before you have time for your first post-baby wax.

Treat yourself to a beautiful, very small, impractical bag
As you will soon find, there is nothing quite as laborious as attempting to leave the house with a baby. Nappies, cream, wipes, bibs, muslins, spare outfits, toys, books and a load of other just-in-case bits – are all stuffed into a skip-sized changing bag. You'll then hobble like a knackered mule with your massive bag from coffee mornings to baby groups, and while it all gets easier and actually very lovely (which you will often hear and it's all completely true), you will still mourn the days of being able to sling a cash card and lipstick into a cute little handbag and skip out the door. So log on to TK Maxx, filter to the designer brands and get something achingly pretty and stupidly expensive you can barely fit a tampon in. Then take it with you everywhere – before you have to stick it in a drawer with your 'good underwear', which will also not see the light of day for a very long time after that baby is born.

Take a day trip ALONE
Your first solo jaunt, to the local Tesco Metro (to buy wine, probably) will be a momentous one. You'll feel as if you've forgotten something and as you pat your pockets and root around in your handbag, you'll suddenly realise that it's your baby whose absence your feeling. It'll be strange – but also very lovely. You're not pushing a buggy, lugging a car seat or trying to breastfeed in a cramped coffee shop while attempting to hold a conversation.

However, as a much-needed new mum, this first trip out, as weirdly wonderful as it will be, will be a rushed one. So, while you can, head to the nearest train station, buy a ticket to somewhere new and lovely, and relish just sitting there, watching the world whizz by the window. Once you have reached your destination, have a delicious three-course lunch – alone. Savour the solitude. Enjoy having both hands free to eat your food and drink a scalding hot beverage, if you so choose. After which, head to the restaurant's loos, plonk yourself down on a lavatory with your favourite magazine nestled on your lap and, if you can manage it, have a beautiful, unhurried dump. Trust me, you will never regret this lost afternoon.

Read several frivolous books that aren't monotonous mum manuals

Once the baby is here, expect to spend a lot of time frantically flipping through a number of paperbacks looking for answers to questions that, as it soon transpires, don't really matter. You and Pete, as you search for explanations for gunky eyes and writhing, restless babies, will frequently ask: 'What does the book say?' And then as more of the dross is recommended/gifted to you, those books will breed into a large, bedside-table tower, each with several earmarked pages, but by and large, mostly unread. Before life is filled with such practical literature which you barely have time to read, get to Waterstones and buy a few trivial, tacky titles. Maybe even a dirty one? Go on, treat yourself. Devour those baby-free, non-guilt-inducing words. Oh, and don't worry, all those tomes of mum doom will not be wasted – they'll be very handy for correcting wonky tables, wedging open sash windows or lobbing at Pete's snoring head.

*

Before I sign off, Heavily Pregnant Me, I want to say one last thing on that subject of guilt. You will spend a lot of your time as a mother battling guilt (you wait until you're a school-gate mum; that shame is *exhausting*), so please, when the baby's out and you spend a lot of your time berating yourself for mourning your independence – don't! Indulge that self-pity a little! Admit you'd give your spleen for a night in the pub! Refuse to deny that barely having time to wipe your arse (not exaggeration, Heavily Pregnant Me) is insanely hideous! It doesn't mean you love your baby less! It just means you're not detrimentally supressing how you feel. And saying it all out loud and proud will also prove a very handy way of warding off the sort of twee twats who did refer to their foetuses as 'bubs' and are most likely lying all over the internet about how 'blessed' they feel…

Now go forth and conquer your pre-baby bucket list. There are peaceful poos to be had.

Love,
Knackered Mum-of-Two Me

Writing a letter to my heavily pregnant self might seem a little pointless (what with me not being Marty McFly and all), but actually, I recommend it. I found it both cathartic and surprising, particularly while unwashed and still in my PJs at two in the afternoon, acknowledging what I missed most.

Listing everything I missed during those independence-depleting newborn days was also a dedicated means of vowing I would never take those things for granted again. A bit like a prisoner serving her time, I was going to relish my liberation with newfound gratitude when I 'got out' (a sketchy analogy I know, but you see where I'm going with this).

Of course, growing up, I never fully grasped how little independence Papa had. With just a year between me and my younger brother, his life, as I've mentioned, pretty much revolved around us and his full-time job. *Channel 4 News* and his newspaper seemed like the only bits of downtime he ever really had.

I asked him once, when I was in my late twenties, if he ever wished he'd met someone else to help raise us. He frowned at me, mid drawing the living-room curtains, slightly annoyed that I'd had the audacity to ask such a pertinent question. 'Don't be silly, Zee! There was no time for all that!' He occupied himself with the curtain and then added plainly: 'And you know, Zeena, there are more women in the world raising children alone. People always ask me, "How did you cope?" I coped the same as a woman bringing up kids by herself! People just care less for her.'

By this point, he'd drawn the other curtain with a flourish, like pulling a metaphorical veil over the matter. It was classic Papa unpretention; his point made, my mind blown, time to move on.

Still, his life living in a 1960s semi-detached just outside Bristol and raising us must have been such a stark contrast to the life he'd known before settling down and becoming a dad. Prior to moving to London for good, he'd travelled to many far-flung places around the world. He'd visited countries including Egypt, Kenya, Turkey, Italy, France, Ireland, Spain, Switzerland, Germany, Holland and Portugal; all before he was twenty-two and at a time when foreign travel was exotic and rare.

When he moved to London, he had a right-old, teetotal knees-up, frequenting Irish folk gigs (still his preferred music genre) all over the city, meeting up with his fellow, now life-long, South African-Indian friends and dating many 'very pretty' nurses. 'Because you know, Zeena, your daddy was good-looking back then,' he's said to me many times with a smile. 'You don't believe me? I'll show you the pictures! I looked like Paul Newman!' Of course, he has never resembled anything remotely close to Paul

Newman, but this is one of Papa's often repeated jokes that my siblings and I have very ungraciously endured over the years.

So, his social life as a full-time single parent couldn't have been more barren by comparison. In fact, it was pretty much non-existent. But, in my memory, he'd never complained about it. Not once. If anything, and please forgive the slight prisoner analogy again, he was so starved of luxuries and time for himself, that he seemed to treasure the smallest of things with enormous enthusiasm.

'Zee! There's a new chocolate called "Galaxy Ripple"! I got one for you, your brother AND me! Yippeee! Not a bad life, eh?'

'Zee! You gonna get jealous! I had a long bath today! It's not a bad life, is it?'

'Zee! A lady in Somerfield gave me a sample of Cup a Soup! And it tasted even better, because it was FREE! Not a bad life!'

Even writing this evokes a huge sense of affection for my dad. I've seen him genuinely excited about something like watching a test match with a small tub of Pringles, or finding that his favourite brand of aubergine purée (one of his staple curry ingredients) is on offer. It's both endearing and humbling. In his eighties, he still derives so much pleasure from his simple daily activities, including breakfasting on toast with fine-cut Seville marmalade, reading (with a highlighter pen) a book about politics and, perhaps most of all, listening to his beloved Radio 4.

In fact, his love affair with Radio 4 and *The Independent* newspaper (although not so much recently as he says he's very disappointed with its sloppy change of editorial direction) did provide him with a sort of 'lobby hobby' in his limited free time. Numerous letters and phone calls, all of political concern, fast became a favourite pastime as he adopted clever pseudonyms to ensure duping the stringent filtering process of both editors and researchers. And I couldn't be prouder of him for it. He couldn't take to the streets of London to demonstrate like he did in his student days, so instead he maximised the power of the telephone and a black Bic – and, like a true nonconformist, he was speaking out by any means necessary!

My most favourite, albeit slightly surreal, 'lobby hobby' moment was when Papa, by that point retired, appeared in the studio audience of BBC1's *Question Time*. Host David Dimbleby, seeing my dad with his hand up, pointed at him and said: 'Yes, a question from the gentleman there with the moustache.' My dad looked around a bit confused. There was a long pause and when David Dimbleby pressed him for his question, he leaned into the boom and said quietly: 'I haven't got a moustache.'

As many a friend will testify, to this day, almost twenty years later, I cannot retell this weird and wonderful story without laughing until I almost pee. (And in case you're wondering, David Dimbleby swiftly apologised, blaming the shadow of the boom for creating the illusion of a moustache.)

Papa's appreciation for the simplest of pleasures came flooding back with complete comprehension why so little meant so much, when I was on maternity leave with Zain.

'I'm so exhausted, Dad,' I remember complaining over the phone once. 'And Zain now won't nap anywhere but on my chest. I had to eat my lunch with one hand!'

'It'll get easier, Zee,' Papa promised sweetly. 'What did you have for lunch?'

'Er, I had a cheese sandwich and crisps,' I replied bemused.

Papa gasped comically: 'Whaat? You had a cheese sandwich AND crisps? NOT A BAD LIFE!'

It was a stock Papa joke, complete with catchphrase. But, as ever, there was some insight behind the jest. It struck me that

Papa's perspective of independence and extravagance, as a single parent, was just redefined – because it had to be! Papa had had years of doing everything by himself, admittedly not the relentless rollercoaster of the baby and toddler years, but certainly most of my and my brother's school years. And while I'm sure adapting to a drastic loss of independence wasn't as simple as placing more value on a cheese sandwich and bag of ready salted, my dear dad, albeit with little choice, acclimatised with extraordinary aptitude.

Papa can still wax lyrical for days about a particularly enjoyable bath or tasty new brand of marmalade. And I am becoming increasingly like him. Today, after dropping Zain and Yasmin at school, I swung by our local Co-op for two pints of semi-skimmed. I also bought a pastry for myself, despite already having breakfast before the school run. I just fancied it. When I got home, I drank two cups of hot tea in succession. I watched an episode of *Come Dine with Me* I'd already seen, but as it was on and it's one of my favourites, I treated myself. (It was the episode where a contestant cheated by deliberately low scoring her rival dinner hosts and then had to redo her scores or face disqualification – a total *CDWM* classic.) My poached-egg lunch will be enjoyed with both hands and a smidgen of ground black pepper. Pete and I might watch a film later. And I have a very promising paperback on my bedside table waiting for me before I retire for some lovely, lengthy kip. These are all emancipations, to this day, I still take enormous pleasure from. Because, actually, when you throw in the insane amount of love I have for my kids…

[pause for dramatic effect]
IT'S NOT A BAD LIFE!

CHAPTER FIVE

Life is All-White on Instagram

'You know, Zeena, I don't even know how to use a stash-tag.'

If you're anything like I was as a new mum, scrolling robotically through various social-media apps on your phone, especially during a late-night feed, has become standard practice. And as I did, you've probably become very familiar with the online mum world targeted largely at you, the new mother. Maybe you've read an open, reassuring letter from a mum blogger, having seen you looking particularly pissed off in a playground, or fit to kill at Jo Jingles? Perhaps you've wandered into a tetchy Mumsnet forum, looking for sleep or teething advice, and observed the virtual foaming at the mouth as members passive-aggressively traded insults? Perchance you've happened on an Instagram account and addictively scrolled through squares of beautiful, middle-class, predominantly white and blonde women who sympathetically say they want to empower you, largely with fashion and a shallow form of feminism? It's this insincere, wily world I want to talk to you about in particular. And while, so far, I have enjoyed a slightly spicy, sarky laugh, this chapter does adopt a more solemn tone. Because this shit really matters…

Now, before this is misconstrued as Instagram bashing, don't get me wrong – I do, on the whole, actually love Instagram. It's often a much kinder, happier place to waste time compared to its feral, fake sister, Facebook. It's true, I am a Generation X mother, and while many millennials refer to themselves as 'children of the internet', I can't ever truly see myself as such. I am a print journalist and have been pretty much my entire working life. So in truth, I'll always feel faintly resentful of an online world that has drastically depleted my industry by the virtue of being free, massively unpoliced and, perhaps most important personally, allowing any ego with an enormous following and the vague ability to string a sentence together to call themselves a writer. (And don't even get me started on the word 'content' in lieu of 'journalism', because seriously, seasons can come and go when I start railing about this.)

Anyway, that all said, I know the worth of social media. The most beneficial to my mind is the voice it provides to people and issues often otherwise unheard. And yes, I'm also aware of how much sanctuary it provided for me when I started my own blog and associated social-media accounts to purge my motherhood miseries. I will always be grateful for this.

My real grievance is with what the British press have now termed 'the mumfluencers'. Admittedly this is a slightly nauseating idiom for, probably unsurprisingly, a mother who is also an influencer on social media. You know the ones I mean – often seen posturing for a #ad, nonchalantly against the backdrop of a beautifully graffitied, urban wall, decked in a @paulsmithdesign metallic bomber, adorned with an effortless blonde top knot, a pop of @lancomeofficial red lipstick and gorgeous, trilby-hatted ('thanks #nextkids!'), hip-side baby? They spend well-documented holidays in scenic, snowy ski settings (#presstrip), and their big, mainly metropolitan homes are #gifted with brands like @farrowandball, @conranshopoffical and @marksandspencer (for the more 'grounded' of influencer, *obvs*).

I know it might seem I'm a little jealous, given I can't rock a top knot and metallic bomber without looking like an oven-ready sumo wrestler. And yes OK, I live in a link-detached new-build

with a lot of Etsy-circa-2009 furnishings. But *please* believe me
when I say these mumfluencers are not your friends. Their bios
might suggest sincere intentions – citing feminism, referencing
'the sisterhood' and even boasting to change preconceived ideas of
how a mum should look – but it's all disingenuous shit. Mothers
like us, with our many mum-related insecurities, are merely the
means to provide them with that privileged lifestyle.

Let me be clear, maternity and breastfeeding fashion is, of
course, a welcome change to the dingy corners of high-street shops,
where a few sad rails of oversized shirts and elasticated clown
trousers hang. But this isn't the 'liberation' these mumfluencers
are referencing. They want to 'free' you from your 'mum coat',
'safe sweater' and 'comfy Converse' (and I'm quoting actual words
here from a newspaper interview with one such mumfluencer, in
regard to typical 'mum dressing', when she launched her Instagram
'brand'). And of course, they're not pressurising you into buying
the colourful clobber credited in the extensively tagged caption
below, and hanging faultlessly from their perfectly petite frames.
No way! They are *helping* you to look less like the time-poor,
knackered eyesore you have become since housing and birthing
human life! Don't you dare suggest it's necessity, not society, that
made you opt for those cheap and nasty leggings – a lack of money,
bigger bodies and barely time to wipe your arse are excuses that
will not be tolerated! Listen, Emily Davison might have thrown
herself under a horse so we could have the right to vote, but these
women are virtually hurling themselves under buggies and prams,
in order to stop exhausted women like YOU swinging by New
Look to buy a terrible-but-practical top!

And, just to stress, while I sit here with all evidence to the
contrary in my 'pull-up' jeans and comfy viscose-blend top, I
do actually enjoy a bit of fashion. It's not a passion for fashion I
take umbrage with, like some festering, misogynistic uncle who
hypocritically sneers at the beauty industry and 'silly women' who

make an effort with their appearance. And I honestly don't object to the kickbacks/freebies/consequent publishing deals/whatever, these blagger-bloggers might receive in exchange for sporting stuff, like urban tourists, against a 'keeping-it-real' Peckham setting. It's genuinely very refreshing to see people other than the likes of Mark Zuckerberg and Cambridge Analytica making cash out of social media – and yes, especially women. However, when exploiting and pressuring a new mum full of self-doubt is all trussed up as emancipation, well, then I'm afraid I do take umbrage.

I have, as you can probably tell, ranted many times about that elite online mum world. I care immensely because to me, it's like having a toxic mate, one who consistently puts you down for their own gain, and honestly, why would anyone willingly subject themselves to that? It's actually quite heart-breaking and has a weird *Handmaid's Tale* subjugation vibe to it.

But as much as I will always protest about how duplicitous and damaging I believe the mumfluencers' brand (being the operative word) of feminism to be, the real issue that galls me is the lack of diversity within that internet space. Those big mum accounts that businesses and brands regularly flock to are so uniformly white, blonde and affluent, there's an almost influencer caricature to them. And the parenting internet sphere, particularly with regards to social media, rarely seems to reflect much beyond them. Platforms in advertising, publishing, the press, television – wherever the mainstream tends to be – have generally, repeatedly, been extended to that white, able-bodied, nuclear-family world.

As I mentioned in the introduction, I want Papa to be the beating heart of this book because he demonstrates perfectly that happy family life can take any form. I'm exhausted with depictions of 'diverse' parenting relegated, bar a little tokenism, to the fringes of mainstream media. A quick google of 'influential families on Instagram' should verify this for anyone in any doubt (I'm sticking with Instagram as an example, as that's where the brand money's at).

The monopoly is very clearly white, beautiful, hugely middle-class mums rocking hair like sunshine and a 'strong lip'. Again, it's the same accounts repeatedly referenced in the 'Top 20 Mumfluencers to Follow on Instagram' style of list many a magazine is partial to. And while the sight of the odd black family, lesbian mums and maybe even a wheelchair might vary the sea of white-blondes and their nuclear families a little, have no doubt, those token accounts are nowhere near as often cited in such lists.

Sometimes, with a gob like mine and particularly being female, it's easy to be perceived as 'drawing up battle lines'. But I don't care. I have no desire to be an influencer (and despite my humble internet space, I have actually been offered a few freebies, including a foreign press trip, all of which I've turned down). But why should I, or anyone else, feel compelled to silently accept that the apparent mega-bucks ecosystem on Instagram is so very clearly weighted heavily in favour of those white, privileged mumfluencers? Make no mistake, that bias, of all the prejudices it encompasses, is largely steeped in racism. Something that revealed itself from those internet quarters in the most explicit and ugly of ways…

The online mum world took quite a dark turn in November 2019. A mumfluencer called Clemmie Hooper, aka 'Mother of Daughters' with close to 700,000 followers, had revealed she'd set up a 'burner' account with a gossip site, in an attempt, she claimed, to defend herself against the many nasty remarks that were said about her there. However, in what she described as 'getting lost in this online world', Clemmie ended up not just bolstering herself but slagging off other mumfluencers and smaller mum accounts too, over the course of eight months and under the alias of Alice in Wanderlust.

Clemmie's alter-ego was exposed when members on the gossip site twigged that 'Alice in Wanderlust' also happened to log on to the forum from the same locations as Clemmie Hooper was posting Instagram pictures from. She was called on it, and she swiftly took to her Insta account to confess and apologise for what she'd done, in an official statement.

It's weird shit, right? And actually, your heart could go out to her – feeling horribly humiliated can resonate with anyone who's blundered in their life, and, you know, who hasn't? However, sympathy might be less forthcoming when you discover what she said about a black British mum blogger, whose account is concerned, it's important to add, specifically with a diverse representation of motherhood in the media: '[She] is really aggressive and always brings it back to race, priveldge [sic] and class because she knows no one will argue with that. It feels like a weapon to silence people's opinions.'

I was horrified. This went way beyond a bit of 'bitching' or 'getting lost in this online world'. This was vile. This was divisive. This was RACISM. Because, seriously, that language is everything. The stereotype of a black woman being 'aggressive' and the objection to a black woman, marginalised and frequently abused, referencing her race too much for her liking? Who, other than a racist, would be motivated to say something like this?

Add to this that Clemmie, a part-time midwife, had featured the same blogger on her podcast just a few months before the shit hit the fan, talking specifically about how black women are five times more likely than white women to die in childbirth thanks to a very apparent healthcare bias, and it all suddenly becomes so much more disturbing. The frightening issues of her being a midwife with those views aside, Clemmie featuring the same black blogger she'd slagged off, on her podcast and subsequently across her social media just reeks of exploitation and tokenism. Talking about race, it would seem, was fine if it was of benefit to Clemmie.

At the point of writing, Clemmie has never actually publicly apologised specifically for those racist comments. After releasing her Instagram-story statement and shutting down her account, nothing more was heard from her. But surely this warranted a response from her fellow mumfluencer mates? The same elite group of white women whose feeds had consistently featured her as they chronicled hanging out together at festivals and press dos, kicking back at some trendy London café and other such Instagrammable events. They'd have to speak out about this? At the very least, it would look unkind not to, and most had shared at some point an inspirational post about the importance of being kind.

So I checked. And aside from those directly targeted by Clemmie's online alias, there was not a word from any of those high-profile mum accounts who had been so publicly associated with her previously. Sure, there were a few lame retweets from one about racism in general being a terrible thing. And another took the time to remind people her account was about fashion not 'politics'. But that was pretty much it from Clemmie's white mumfluencer mates; Clemmie's name was suddenly like Voldemort in *Harry Potter*.

Obviously, there were many, myself included, who weren't going to be silent on this matter. We challenged this across our own more modest platforms. A few followers and accounts even directly addressed individual mumfluencer accounts and asked why they were saying nothing. A black fitness blogger even challenged Clemmie directly, while her Mother of Daughters account was still active, about her racist remarks, and, as a result, was set on by a chunk of Clemmie's devoted followers who reported and consequently prompted Instagram to shut down the fitness blogger's account. She was literally silenced for daring to criticise the queen of mumfluencers! Thankfully though, through social media harnessed for the power of good and enough angry people lobbying, her account was rightly reinstated (with reportedly no apology from Instagram incidentally).

A lot of the argument from Clemmie's loyal camp was about concerns for her mental health. She must be 'unwell' or 'not herself' to have behaved in such a way, and of course, accusations of 'weaponising' mental health would not be cool here. But repeatedly reading this line of defence was just exhausting. It feels like every time a white person is caught racially abusing someone of colour, particularly when it's vastly exposed on the internet, this excuse will be wheeled out in a bid to portray the perpetrator as the victim. And of course, as that fitness blogger can testify, we know who often winds up depicted as the perpetrator...

Soon, of course, after a flurry of headlines largely describing Clemmie as a 'troll' or an 'online bully' – but rarely a racist – everything blew over. Clemmie closed her Instagram account, those mumfluencers resumed their hashtag lives and not much more was really said on the matter. Those hurt and angry were just left to simply accept, as is generally, sadly, the case, that another racist incident, bar a few dissenting voices, had pretty much slipped by unchallenged.

Then, during the pandemic of 2020, a protest swept Instagram in early June on the back of the death of George Floyd, an African-American man viciously and sickeningly killed by a white Minneapolis policeman, 'apprehending' him for alleged counterfeit cash use, by kneeling on his neck. The campaign in question was originally organised within the music industry, titled The Show Must Be Paused, with a call for business to halt for the day, as a show of unity with the Black Lives Matter movement and outrage at the killings of not just George Floyd, but fellow African-Americans Ahmaud Arbery and Breonna Taylor, both also recently losing their lives at the hands of barbaric police brutality.

Social-media platforms filled with plain black squares as a mark of solidarity, and soon the black square, like a flag at half-mast, was adopted globally by those wanting to show their support. There were hashtags citing Black Lives Matter, BIPOC (black, indigenous and people of colour) accounts supported and resources shared, and white people in particular were promising to educate themselves and use their privilege to be the best possible antiracism ally they could. It was known as Blackout Tuesday and I found it extraordinary, along with many angry worldwide protests, to sense such a massive collective and engaged response, not just about those horrific deaths and police brutality, but about fighting racism everywhere.

Now, as I've probably made quite clear, I'm not exactly a fan of those mumfluencer accounts, and for the sake of my blood pressure, I generally tend to steer well and truly clear of their platforms. But now, on the back of their deafening silence with regard to Clemmie's racist remarks in November 2019, I had to know: would they be among those posting black squares to their grids, referencing Black Lives Matter, spouting the ethics of antiracism? Surely, without addressing the racist in their mum midst they'd previously ignored, they couldn't sincerely do that?

But they did. All of them. All those who had said nothing back in November were now promising to always speak out against racism and suggesting their respective massive followings should do the same. Still no mention of Clemmie, however. No reference to those hurtful, *racist* words they could now take the opportunity to call out, alongside these well-worded oaths. No open remorse for their lack of antiracism allyship then.

I was livid. How *dare* they? On the back of throat-choking, murderous racism, it looked very much to me like they'd seized an opportunity; superficially and greedily showing up now for a hot-button issue, much like they did with feminism.

I was as angry with their hypocrisy as I was with Clemmie's comments, and once again, I said as much across my social media.

'How fucking dare you' I blasted in a post, pointing out their silence in November 2019, their failure still to condemn those comments and the distinct bandwagon-hopping feel to their Blackout Tuesday posts. The post engaged with hundreds of people (small fry for a mumfluencer but fairly significant for a provincial pleb like me), and soon after, lifestyle magazine *Marie Claire* picked up on the post. They invited me to write a piece for them specifically about the mumfluencers' lack of real allyship. Knowing this was an opportunity to address this for such an esteemed, widely read title (one I'd long admired and dreamed about writing for), I said yes please before they could change their minds.

I decided to pen an open letter to those mumfluencers and I'm sharing that letter here as it really did sum up everything I was feeling about that world, that I still feel…

Dear White 'Mumfluencers',

My name is Zeena Moolla. Like you, I am a part of the online mum world, albeit I occupy a far less frequented space on the internet, with a blog called Word to the Mothers. I apologise for the unsolicited nature of this address, but I felt we needed to talk…

Let me start positively. I think it's great, as you posted your black squares for #blackouttuesday, that you asserted black lives matter. I think it's lovely that you quoted from very credible books about race. And I think it's brilliant you took the time to list recommended resources to help your respective, massive followings educate themselves and their children, in the ways of antiracism.

But otherwise, frankly, and I make no apology for my angry caps here: HOW DARE YOU.

Remember in November last year when your fellow white 'mumfluencer' Clemmie Hooper, aka 'Mother of Daughters', made racist remarks under an online alias about other influencers? Remember how she accused a mum blogger, concerned specifically with encouraging a diverse representation of motherhood across all media, of weaponising race? Remember her vernacular? 'Aggressive'. 'Social-climber'. 'Shady'. Remember how then, YOU, her online gang of elite, all-white 'mumfluencers' said NOTHING to condemn it?

'But I know her IRL,' protested one of you, when you were taken to task by a tweeter brave enough to challenge you for still following and being 'brand associated' with Clemmie. 'I don't do politics,' said another of you, pushed after days of silence to address the woman who'd previously peppered your feed, as you'd holidayed and hung out in beautiful, gifted clothes together. 'No comment,' was the response my journalist-friend received from every single high-profile influencer and blogger when she tried and failed to find just one of you to speak out about Clemmie's comments.

So, I'm curious, why were your voices so loud and proud last week? Why say stuff like:

'We need to speak up and know that speaking up is only the start?'

'We have to talk about racism and support marginalised communities.'

'Racism should not exist and I will not avoid talking about it for fear of getting it wrong.'

Where was this 'support' last November? Where was this vow to 'talk', when you stood mutely by the perpetrator of racism? Why have you YET to 'speak up' directly about Clemmie's racist remarks? Because, however poignant and sincerely meant those #blackouttuesday words were, they are hollow without acknowledging your prior lack of allyship you're so vocal with now.

Maybe you're wondering why someone like me is quite so angry with you? Allow me to elaborate for you…

I'm half-Indian, don't particularly look it, but am it and very proud of it I am too. My name is Arabic as my father is Indian-Muslim and although I'm atheist, I'm very proud of this aspect of my heritage as well. And while I'm completely aware of my own privilege – I am fair-skinned, middle class and lead a pretty quiet, suburban life – I know what it's like to be 'othered' and subjected to racism. Believe me, this shit cuts very deep.

Some of my experiences for you:

The time, as a teenager, someone telephoned my house, racially abused my dad and hung up. The time a girl in my year threatened to 'wait' for me after school, because I had the nerve to object to the racist 'jokes' I regularly received from her friends. The time some random American bloke, while I was on holiday in Ireland, angrily informed me in a bar that the 'Moss-lems' had declared 'war on the world' and as such, I owed him some sort of explanation. The time a flatmate's boyfriend told me he couldn't stand 'p*kis' particularly the 'Muslim ones', and when I angrily challenged him, told me I could fuck off (out of my own flat!), if I didn't like it. And there are other experiences I could list, largely from my school years, some of them too personal and hurtful to share.

So, you see, for me and many other people, this is all too familiar; Clemmie, the bully, the rest of you, the entourage the bully surrounds herself with.

Look, I understand that we all get stuff wrong and make mistakes on occasion. But we need to own those mistakes, apologise *specifically* for them and then look at how we can make direct amends. It's not too late for you to do this. Although, I have to say, your intentions don't look particularly promising when you disable the comments under your black squares, or restrict the visibility of comments calling out your hypocrisy to leave just the praise from dedicated followers, applauding the positive use of your platforms. To my more cynical mind, it looks very much to me like you're using your platforms to exploit a campaign. It looks to me like you're commodifying antiracism for your respective brands.

Before I sign off, I want to clarify why, apart from Clemmie, I haven't named any of you specifically. That's because this is about ALL of you. All you white 'mumfluencers' who had the opportunity last November, relevant entirely to your online world, to demonstrate across your mammoth platforms, just how antiracist you claim to be – and you chose to be silent.

Until you address that, you are as complicit with racism now as you were then.

Zeena

As I wrote that letter for *Marie Claire*, I had to stop to cry. Even now, I'm blinking back sharp, angry tears. I'll never stop being furious. As I told an Instagram follower testily asking why I was still talking about it, some of us won't stop talking about it – because we can't. It'll never be 'old news' or simply 'in the past'. It will always hurt.

School, as I'd mentioned in that open letter, is where my encounters with racism largely stem from. I grew up in a small suburban town during the 1980s and attended schools with very few pupils of black, Asian and minority ethnic backgrounds. It was while I was at comprehensive school that I became really familiar with just how routine and accepted racism could be. Some of the tamer comments for you:

- *'Will you see your dad here?'* [Said to me on a school trip to the Sikh temple in Bristol, albeit my father is a Muslim.]
- *'Oh dearie-dearie me!'* [Said to me with a head wobble and caricature Indian accent, by the same boy on a regular, 'hilarious' basis.]
- *'Why can't you take a joke?'* [Said to me by a classmate after he'd asked me why my dad had the skin colour of excrement (although that wasn't the word he used, of course).]

It makes my heart pound with upset and anger every time I recall these memories. I had cried in front of those kids at school, explained why they weren't 'just words' and, eventually, grassed to a teacher. All of which resulted in a handful of 'apology letters' from a few boys in my class, followed by a lot of resentment and that girl I mentioned in my *Marie Claire* piece who threatened to 'get' me after school as a mark of solidarity to her friends. (Incidentally, she never did 'get' me in the end – she'd changed her mind because she was going to the fun fair in town for the week, instead. I guess I have the dodgems to thank for dodging a hiding.)

However, I do want to point out that while I can never forget those experiences, I can forgive. While I know not everyone would share my views (and as I said in my *Marie Claire* letter, I'm completely aware that my fair skin gives me a far more fortunate perspective of racism and I would never want to pretend otherwise), for me, a genuine apology means an awful lot.

I'll never forget one of those lads who'd had to write me an apology letter approaching me in the local pub when I was about nineteen and very awkwardly but sweetly saying sorry for, in his words, 'being a dick at school'. 'I didn't really know they were racist jokes at the time. I do now and I'm really sorry,' he said.

It blew me away. He was genuinely nervous, and I could see it had taken guts for him to address this with me. Would it change how I felt when I recalled those 'jokes'? Probably not. But his apology (not forced by a teacher) told me he accepted responsibility and the onus wasn't on me to 'change my reaction' to it all (as was said a lot to me at the time). I really appreciated his effort and remorse and said as much.

I didn't tell Papa about those incidents while I was at school. I didn't want to hurt him or for him to worry about me. I did, though, end up telling him about some of those school experiences before writing that piece for *Marie Claire*, explaining it had been commissioned on the back of a racist catalyst of comments on Instagram (the latter of which, to be honest, took some effort thanks to his bad hearing and lack of digital understanding).

'You never told me about what happened at school before, Zee,' Papa said quietly as we chatted in the summer sun of his back garden.

'It wasn't an everyday occurrence, Dad. And I dealt with it.' I was trying to sound breezy but was struggling to look Papa in the eye.

He shrugged and gave me a weary look. 'There's always been racism in the world, Zee. And how people can say things like "oh, that's terrible in this day and age", I don't know! This day and age is when people are giving power to *openly* racist governments! If we can't expect an apology from them, don't expect one from those women on social media!'

I sipped my tea, nodding in complete agreement as Papa continued to list reams of global racism, both past and present, which much of the world has been happy to turn a blind eye to. Every word he said was passionate and true. When he'd finished, he pulled up his surgical sock to cover his bad leg he'd absent-mindedly been scratching.

After a pause, he looked at me with a puzzled expression: 'You know, Zeena, I don't even know how to use a stash-tag.'

God LOVE him.

CHAPTER SIX

Signs You're a Mum in Need of a Break

'You know, Zeena, if you need a break, just go to Iceland!'

I am writing this chapter while on a short break in the Gower, South Wales. If you're unfamiliar, it's a gorgeous part of the world – golden soft sandy beaches, breath-taking limestone cliffs and the most delicious ice cream (next to kulfi), I've ever tasted. However, today it pissed down, meaning we didn't leave the lovely little holiday cottage we're staying in until we ventured out for fish and chips early evening. We played board games. We watched films. We ate a lot of beige snacks.

As I sit here on the bed writing, exhausted from repeatedly telling my kids to 'pack it in', and bickering with Pete about who was responsible for neglecting to do the dishwasher (*he* should have done it), I can hear the rain lashing against the window. At the foot of the bed lies an already overflowing laundry bag which will need emptying into the machine pretty much as soon we're home (and by which point there will likely be at least two, maybe three, loads to do). It took me almost a day to pack and I still forgot my toothbrush. I also didn't bring enough bread for the many rounds of sandwiches we take to the beach, meaning I have had to dash to the overpriced beachfront shop for some emergency sliced white (what was I thinking bringing one loaf for a family of four? I'm not Jesus!). Heavy rain is forecast for most of the week, the nearest pub has closed down and I'm pretty sure I passed a sign on the way down here for scheduled roadworks, which could result in a taxing, tetchy journey home.

Clearly, family holidays are for fools, right? WRONG! I have never craved and treasured a getaway more than I have since becoming a mother! And in the run-up to this break, something as simple as choosing a new swimming costume for Yasmin or buying a Kellogg's Variety Pack (a holiday tradition) gave me a little buzz knowing that soon, we'd all be waking up somewhere else, happily sniffing different air like little acclimatising hamsters. Because at least twice a year, my surroundings can start to feel oppressive – and it's a different kind of suffocation to that I might have encountered in my child-free life when a hectic work life or bad break-up had me logging on to lastminute.com. It's a *Groundhog Day* desperation. It's a simple need to change location, rest my eyes on pretty backdrops and not feel hemmed in by the overfamiliarity of both a relentless routine and my home.

While I was on both maternity leaves in particular, signs I needed a break became increasingly apparent as my behaviour became a little neurotic. I'd find myself, perhaps during a sleepy feed or a labour-intensive nappy change, fixating on a broken drawer handle I'd been meaning to mention to Pete for months. I might genuinely get quite stressed at the level of noise from the glass-shattering recycling truck, landing in our street bang on nap time. And I even once found myself, slightly ghoulishly, watching the postie breezily delivering mail in the neighbourhood, jealously pondering on what sort of self-indulgent activities (like having a cup of tea or a beautiful nap) lay ahead of him when he'd finish his round.

Perhaps you are familiar with this? Maybe you're feeling ready to pack up the contents of your home and enough baby paraphernalia to set up your own branch of Mothercare? If you're still unsure you're on the cusp of a claustrophobic crisis, perhaps this might help determine if you are a mum in need of a holiday…

Signs you're a mum in need of a holiday!

Since becoming a mum, is your idea of a break catching your breath on the landing or having enough time to cut your toenails? Do you feel positively Mediterranean slinging a bit of feta in your shopping trolley and having a siesta (or rather passing out from exhaustion) on the couch while your baby naps? It could be you are suffering from a well-known condition called MINOAH – Mum in Need of a Holiday. Don't worry, it's not serious (in fact, it's entirely made up for the purposes of this piece), but urgent treatment is required – sun, sea and a shitload of wine. In case you are still unsure you have it, here are eight more symptoms of MINOAH…

1. You booked your last break through Teletext – after 'setting the video' for Dynasty

If the last time you went anywhere involving an overnight stay was when your hair was backcombed and you knew who was at number one in the 'hit parade', then let's be honest, it's time for a decent holiday. No more but-it's-just-so-hard-when-you-have-kids excuses – you really don't want to be that mum who thinks a can of Lilt in the park is exotic. But before you book your static caravan, you should know a few things first: no one is pushing the pineapple anymore, they don't do Jazzercise in the pool and you will find most end-of-the-pier comedians signing on, lamenting the days before Operation Yewtree.

2. You find yourself slumped at the end of the day, mouth open, in front of CBeebies for over half an hour before changing the channel

True, this is pretty standard stuff for most knackered mums and is up there with boiling a kettle for no reason at all and mindlessly changing a bone-dry nappy. However, you know it's time to dig out the luggage and lilo when you find yourself watching, without moving, whole episodes of *In the Night Garden,* and wondering aloud to your half-lidded partner slumped next to you: 'Do you think all creators of children's telly are drug casualties suffering from hallucinogenic flashbacks?'

3. You start thinking about that bottle of Rioja around 10 a.m.

To be fair, after a night of squirting syringes of Calpol down reluctant gullets, humming 'Twinkle Twinkle' while lying on the floor next to a restless cot and then *still* rising before 6 a.m. on the back of approximately twenty minutes' sleep, you've pretty much completed a full working day by 10 a.m. But when you're on the countdown to a post-witching-hour tipple before you've even finished your Marmite on toast, it's maybe time to step away from the wine rack and load up the roof rack. Just don't forget the wine…

4. You're in danger of getting rickets, given the most exposure you get to the sun is walking to Tesco – from its adjacent car park

There's no denying slinging kids into a car is generally far more appealing than the prospect of wobbling down the road with a cumbersome buggy and sighing at a toddler: 'Come on! Leave that stone where it is! No, I don't want to see the cat poo that looks like an elephant.' Perhaps, though, it's time to park the car (yes that's very cleverly both literal *and* metaphoric) and get a decent dose of vitamin D that's not in tablet form. Treat yourself to a cheeky jaunt where you can chide 'Come on! Leave that stone where it is! No, I don't want to see the cat poo that looks like an elephant' in a slightly nicer, new environment.

5. You find yourself envying the paperboy for a job that involves a degree of travel

Look at him, arms swinging either side of his fluorescent, cross-body messenger bag, resentfully stuffing the free rag into letterboxes before swaggering back down the path like a gorilla. He's free to roam around the neighbourhood, do a wheelie, eat a bag of Monster Munch with *both* hands – he doesn't know he was born, that pubescent paperboy prick! Such inner monologue running through your head while observing a person more liberated than yourself – someone who isn't stuck indoors with babies and barf clamped to their hair – needs addressing. It's time to stop staring at the paperboy from behind the nets and take a sanity-saving trip, pronto! Before someone calls the police and you find yourself holidaying courtesy of Her Majesty's Prison Service.

6. You habitually forget what you've walked into a room for

You know you've become your dad when you shuffle upstairs, scan the room you've just walked into and mutter to yourself: 'Now, what did I come up here for?' Then, as you slowly recall it was your glasses that prompted your pensioner plod-like ascension, you ramble room to room getting more vexed hunting for the specs you literally had in your hand just a moment ago. Finally, just as you're about to lumber dejectedly back downstairs, you tentatively pat your face and, feeling like a massive twat, discover you've been wearing them the entire time. Get thee on thy jollies, Grandma!

7. You are fixated, a little more than is healthy, with the man across the road's recycling bin

It's a sure-fire sign your world has become too small when you find yourself trailing your indifferent other half around the house, relaying the man across the road's recycling bin sins of unflattened juice cartons and offending mixed matter in his green box. Similarly, your wearied spouse most likely couldn't give a tiny gnat's crap that the woman with three cars has parked in your spot again, or that the despondent teenager on the checkout at Tesco looked at your bawling baby in a funny way, or that the grumpy postman knocked really loudly, probably, most definitely, on purpose at nap time. Get a grip! Get away!

8. You haven't got the energy to row

Babies and barneys are as routine as midwife visits, once the sleep deprivation kicks in. How can you *not* seethe and hiss a little at each other when an insomniac giraffe gets more sleep than you? So when you begin to casually observe, without even so much as a whimper of objection, your partner pretending to still be asleep when it's his turn to settle the baby, or worse, replacing the toilet paper with the loose side facing in, it's a sign your fatigue has seriously tipped over into the dark side. It's clear you're in need of sandy, soggy nappies, overpriced plastic beach toys and many, many sticky ice-cream kisses. The stuff of lovely, long-lasting and yes, OK, rose-tinted memories. Altogether now: 'You missed the exit, you idiot!'

*

Yes, the energy to row well and truly returns on a family holiday.

'Did you remember to bring the swimming nappies?'

'Did *you* remember to bring the swimming nappies?'

'I said junction 22 not junction 21!'

'You need a degree in engineering to assemble this bloody tent!'

'I'm NOT criticising your parenting. I'm merely suggesting that packing twenty-seven bottles of Malbec, but not his stuffed elephant without which he screams like a crazed chimpanzee and refuses to sleep, was perhaps a bit misjudged?'

Honestly, though, if you do decide to book a break, might I advise you, do take a lot of wine? Work out how much you think you'll need – then double it. I've already had to do a booze run to the overpriced beachfront shop, and it breaks my heart to tell you that the wine I bought was completely undrinkable. And I have never before discovered an undrinkable wine. Seriously, I won't be making that mistake again, I can assure you.

When I told Papa we were going to the Gower for a holiday, he said what he always says: 'Why do you need to leave home? You can have a holiday at home for nothing!' Papa, despite his many travels in his younger years, has not really relished leaving home, even to travel from Bristol to London, since his fifties. 'I like being home, Zee,' he'll say, lifting the lever on his armchair and elevating his feet. 'I've got everything I need here – marmalade, *Channel 4 News*, Radio 4. It's not a bad life!'

He's only half joking. Home, the 1960s semi-detached ten miles out of Bristol that he's lived in for over forty years, is well and truly where his heart is. And simple pleasures (although that marmalade does really need to be of a good Seville quality) genuinely make him happiest. So, if you've concluded you're not ready to embark on a break – and who can blame you when babies are not exactly great for getting pissed by the pool with – perhaps a Papa-style staycation (flips off the global pandemic of 2020 for the rise of this dreadful word) could appeal…

How to have 'not a bad life' at home

Go to Iceland!

No, not the country, home to the Northern Lights and Björk – the supermarket of course! Papa's a big fan. His daily constitutional will nearly always involve a trip to either Iceland or Tesco, often both. But it's Iceland that hits the happy spot the most. A trip to the town precinct with my pop is not complete without venturing in to check the yellow-stickered clearance shelf, or to see if the frozen prawns are on offer. And why anyone would do their full shop in somewhere as fancy-pants as Waitrose is beyond him. On entering his home with just one bag of shopping from there, you'd better brace yourself for the inevitable: 'HAVE YOU WON THE LOTTERY?'

These days, I'm very much my father's daughter when it comes to relishing a supermarket trip. Before meeting Pete, when I was living alone, a trip to Tesco was a necessary bind, something I approached with a certain amount of dread as I resentfully slung packets of pasta and a sad, small sliced loaf into my trolley. Since becoming a mum, even eight years on, a trip to Tesco alone now sees me burst through those automatic doors high kicking and twirling like Hugh Jackman in *The Greatest Showman*. The bright fluorescent lights, excessive square footage of colourful, enticing foods, the cooling breeze of the frozen-food cabinets, THE WINE AISLE – oh my God! What's not to love? Forget online shopping! This place is Disneyland for the solo parent shopper! And should you require a slightly more distinctive holiday feel to the experience, you could always, while in shorts and flip-flops, try to haggle, very loudly, with the shelf stacker restocking the spice aisle?

Speak on the phone to an overseas relative like it's 1986

If you're a 1970s/80s child of at least one foreign parent, perhaps thickly accented and heralding from some far-off land, you will likely remember what it's like when a relative from overseas rang. It went something like this in our house:

[The phone on the landing rings. Papa answers.]
'Hello?'

[Pause. Papa proceeds to shout.]

'AH! *WALAIKUM SALAM! KEM CHHE BHAI*? HOW ARE YOU? *JEE, ALHAMDULILLAH*, THANK YOU!'

[I turn up *Brookside* because Papa is shouting so loud.]

'WHAT? *BHAI*! IT'S A VERY BAD LINE! I CAN'T HEAR YOU? WHAT? OH, YES, ALL WELL THANK YOU. WHAT? I DIDN'T CATCH THAT, *BHAI*? THIS LINE IS VERY BAD! THIS MUST BE COSTING YOU A FORTUNE, *BHAI*?'

[Still Papa and his brother persist and several other South African family members then take turns to talk to Papa, also shouting over the top of each other in a similar chaotic manner.]

It was like a little bit of South African family in our house for the duration of that loud, happy phone call and, also, usually *Brookside*.

So try it? If, like many modern households, you no longer have a landline, simply place your mobile phone in the hallway or on the landing. Then, when it rings, get someone else to answer it and shout irritably: 'It's for you!' Next, proceed to bellow excitably for half an hour while the person on the other end makes crackling noises and speaks with a slight delay. It's both nostalgic *and* exotic! You need never leave the house again…

Go to an airport really, really, early

(OK, so this suggestion, while not strictly a staycation idea, is a more shameless ruse to share a childhood memory for sheer hilarity…)

When I was about eight, we missed our flight to South Africa. Long story short, a lot of terrible traffic between Reading and Heathrow saw us arriving at Departures around the time our flight was due to take off. Albeit we were able to fly out the next day, it was an experience that scarred poor Papa for life. After that, any impending flight (pretty much always to South Africa) would see us abruptly woken from our slumbers around 4 a.m., arriving at our terminal at about 7 a.m. – to wait for a flight that wasn't due to depart until approximately three in the afternoon! By the time our flight was called, we'd bustle to the gate proffering our boarding passes like castaways desperate for rescue to a flight attendant who'd barely had time to take her coat off.

To recreate this illusion of foreign travel as per much of my childhood, arrive at the airport at some horrid hour to be greeted by a depressing sea of aluminium roller shutters on practically everything that could feasibly offer any form of entertainment. Then hang about for several hours, within the confines of a hard, hostile chair, sniffing perfume samples in discarded magazines, eating endless home-brought snacks wrapped in kitchen towel, while staring forlornly at the departures board for a flight so far into the future, a clairvoyant would doubt its existence. This should knock the desire to holiday abroad right out of you.

Buy some obscure ingredients and let them go grotesquely out of date

When I was growing up, often the sign of a special occasion looming or that there'd been a particularly good deal on in Bristol Sweet Mart was a cupboard well stocked with guava juice. Just a whiff of it always put me in mind of the pungent, balmy, guava-scented air that engulfs the family house my father grew up in. Its aroma alone makes me happy and immediately crave a tandoori chicken roti-wrap or some bunny chow (a South African-Indian dish of a hollowed-out loaf filled to the brim with curry – really ugly but really delicious, I swear). However, most of this abundance of guava juice was destined for a life, at least ten years over its best-before date, at the back of the cupboard.

Out-of-date guava juice in lieu of a holiday might sound a bit shit (and, well, that's because it kind of is). But, like the bar of creamed coconut that would sit in the fridge door for several years, and the approximately 10,000 tins of patra (yam leaves) living in the larder way beyond their expiry date, it brought a little imported sunshine and signs of South African life into our home.

So if you'd like to relive a little of this magic Papa-style, first, go to the part of town where the South Asian shops are – the kind that might sell traditional Indian sweetmeats (which are an acquired taste and one I've yet to acquire). Next, purchase far too much of one particular, hard-to-source product (packets of ajwain seeds, pickled okra, and jars of achar that could render you unconscious are all good options). Then use just one of these items, while the remainder of your purchases sit untouched until some archaeological excavation unearths them to be featured in a museum, alongside a full bottle of Fine Fare powdered toilet cleaner purchased in 1979, still sitting in the downstairs loo.

Sing Indian pop songs in the bath loudly and badly and proudly

The soundtrack to my 1980s childhood, like that of many of my friends, entailed a lot of taped Top 40 hits, recorded studiously (and, of course, illegally) every Sunday, abruptly hitting 'stop' when Radio 1 DJ Bruno Brookes would interject with some inane patter. A few friends and I would then enjoy lounging around my bedroom reading magazines like *Blue Jeans* and *My Guy*, singing along, largely to the choruses of my unlawful Top 40 recording. So far, a pretty happy memory, right? Well, this rose-tinted recollection is sadly stained by one particular, seemingly innocuous incident…

One lazy, 1980s Saturday afternoon, a friend and I had returned from the precinct, fresh from our magazine and sweet run, to my geometric-styled bedroom, ready to head bop to a little Level 42 while ripping out our fillings with lemon bonbons. As my friend reclined, already steaming into her *Jackie*, I hit 'play' on the cassette player and flopped on my bed ready to tuck into a photo-story, likely about a cheating boyfriend or a girl living in the shadow of her more popular friend.

Suddenly, a shrill voice from my cassette player jolted my friend and me mid bonbon. '*Abhi nahi! Abhi nahi!*' sang the shrill voice to, what my scared senses slowly made out to be, a very jangly version of 'Honey, Honey' by Abba. It was Papa's Hindi Abba hits cassette. This was a firm favourite of his, especially for bath times when he'd pull the cassette player into the bathroom via an extension lead on the landing and sing hideously at the top of his voice, while I silently prayed the bathroom window was shut.

'What is THAT?' My friend was clutching her chest in mock shock.

'Er, nothing… It's, um, my dad's…' I stammered, scrambling up from the bed, desperate to shut off the music so alien to my friend, she was now gasping with incredulous laughter.

'God, he's so embarrassing – I can't believe he listens to that crap.' I rolled my eyes, secretly irritated by how amused she was, as I badly feigned laughter until she finally resumed her copy of *Jackie*.

Now, I can't deny it, that cassette did sound faintly ridiculous. Between the pitch, jaunty pace and the tape's overuse warbling in places, it sounded a bit like a Hindi Minnie Mouse on acid. However, looking back, what bothers me is not the mortifying cartoon nature of the music, or how the cassette ended up in my twin-deck stereo in the first place (which, by the way, I still firmly believe had something to do with my younger brother). I don't even begrudge my friend's reaction to the cassette. It's me and my horrible shame that makes me wince most.

Papa loved that cassette! He'd sing loud and proud because it lifted his spirits. His heritage, culture and family were all contained within that battered c-90. I could never say that about Level 42!

Level 42 were crap! I should have never hissed shushes at my dad as I passed the bathroom door. And I regret miserably dissing the music that transported him every bath time, simply because my teenage angst made me resent being different.

Perhaps, to help appease some of my teen guilt, I could persuade you to find similar joy with such bath-time transportation? Next time you have a bath, take a radio into the bathroom while observing all health and safety measures as Papa did [coughs]. Tune into an Asian station, one preferably playing old-fashioned Bollywood hits, and then sing without any inhibition whatsoever, imagining yourself twirling in a bright, beautiful lehenga choli while Salman Khan smoulders nearby in a bad leather jacket. Bath-time Bollywood: *Ek bura jeevan nahin hai*! (Which in Hindi means… wait for it… IT'S NOT A BAD LIFE!)

I'm not sure what ever happened to that Hindi Abba hits tape (and I swear its disappearance had nothing to do with me), but I've found 'Abhi Nahi' on YouTube. I vow to not only bathe singing along to that song with glorious gusto, but also to teach my children to do the same. Because I want them to experience nothing but pride in every aspect of their Indian heritage.

Of course, I realise a teenager resenting any difference about themselves is not uncommon. But when you feel alienated and ridiculed because of your marginalised ethnicity, it's exceptionally hostile. It's also completely intended that way. And when you are first made aware of this, it shapes every similar encounter in your life thereafter.

I want to change tone slightly here to share one particularly young memory I have, because I think it illustrates this point entirely. I want to present a wider context as to why someone like myself might appear at times so dogged and defensive:

January 1983, Papa treated me and my brother to a pantomime at the Bristol Hippodrome. I think it was *Jack and the Beanstalk*, starring end-of-the-pier comedian Tom O'Connor as the narrator.

My brother and I were sitting either side of Papa, enjoying the show and the packet of sweets we were each allowed to eat throughout.

During one act, Tom O'Connor, for some bizarre reason my memory can't help me with, then used road signs as a means of storytelling and it was clear this was the 'bit-blue-for-the-dads' part of the pantomime. So, for a couple of painful examples, the 'humps ahead in the road' sign was held upside down to look like a pair of breasts, and the 'wind' road sign pertained to some pitiful punchline about flatulence. The one I vividly remember him holding up was the 'roadworks' sign, which, as you probably know, is a black figure digging into what looks like a pile of rubble.

'Where do you think he's from?' called out Tom O'Connor in what felt like a very staged moment. Without a heartbeat, someone in the audience fired back: 'St Paul's!'

The laughter was deep and deafening around us as a lot of dads in particular, previously visibly bored and checking their watches, roared their approval.

I didn't get it. I smiled bemusedly at my dad and asked: 'Why are they laughing?'

Papa's face was solemn. He was the only parent around us not laughing. 'It's not funny,' he said, shaking his head. 'St Paul's is a mainly Afro-Caribbean area in Bristol. They think it's hilarious because the sign looks like a black person.'

My smile faded quickly. I surveyed the crowd. Papa's was the only brown face I could see. I caught the eye of a dad laughing next to me who looked past me and at my dad. He saw my dad's unhappy face, which only seemed to amuse him more. It all felt horribly alienating. In our vicinity was a sea of white families, who had probably explained that joke to their children in a totally different context to the way Papa had, happily passing on their discriminatory, jeering humour and keeping that spite alive.

Whenever I think of that memory, while I can still feel the way it stung, I also feel so much pride for Papa. He could have laughed along instead of so visibly displaying his disapproval – after all, he's not Afro-Caribbean, he's Asian. But that joke hurt us too. When he stood on those doorsteps in 1950s London seeking a place to stay and was turned away by a gesture to a 'no coloureds' sign, the message was as clear as it was in South Africa: privilege belonged to white people. And anyone other than white would be made to feel ostracised. There's nothing remotely funny about that. It's cruel. It's *racist*. And there, sitting in that pantomime audience in 1983, Papa was going to make sure that we, his ten-year-old daughter and nine-year-old son, understood that that 'joke' and those bellowing laughs we felt so horribly uncomfortable with were incited entirely by the same racism.

Like Papa, I fully intend to raise my kids, with a concerted and conscious effort, to call out racism however lone their voices might be. I also want them to champion their Indian-Muslim background. I've overheard both Zain and Yasmin brag separately to friends, 'I'm a quarter Asian,' and each time I felt a little choked. (And while I want them to feel pride in their Devonshire-Methodist and Irish-Catholic heritage as well, let's be honest here, white Europeanness is rarely subjected to bigotry in the same way.)

I want my kids to explain with self-esteem that their names are Muslim. I want them to fully understand, discuss and celebrate everything about their Indian and South African roots. I want them to sing loud and proud – Papa-style.

CHAPTER SEVEN

How to do Romance Post-Kids

'You know, Zeena, you mustn't bully Peter – he's a good boy.'

36-year-old female seeks boyfriend

Must be kind. Must be sincere. Must be emotionally intelligent. Must be monogamous. Must have a sense of humour. Must be smart. Must be smart enough to like smart women.

Must not take washing home to Mother. Must not wish to meet a woman just like Mother. Must not live with Mother.

Must not say shit like: 'I just don't find women that funny.' Must not say shit like: 'You're not that pretty to be that picky.' Must not say shit like: 'What I love about our relationship is that we're so casual.' Must not say the latter in an attempt to exit a relationship and pork someone else.

Must not be one of those weird misogynists who dates women solely to dump them. Must not be one of those weird misogynists who loses all respect for women he sleeps with. Must not be one of those weird misogynists seeking a 'shy' woman, when he actually means he wants a woman who doesn't challenge him in any way, shape or form. Must not be a misogynist, full stop.

Must not remove a chunk of lamb from a Sunday roast caught between the front teeth, using a travel card as floss, while on a date. Must not then dump said travel card, complete with masticated meat, on the table, in front of still-eating date.

Must not assume all single women in their thirties are trying to frogmarch men up the aisle. Must not assume all single women in their thirties are looking for men to father their babies. Must not assume himself to be Big in Sex and the City.

Must not get snide and sulky because a woman doesn't reciprocate his affections. Must not get snide and sulky because a woman does reciprocate the affections of another. Must not get snide and sulky ever.

Must not be a very senior TV twat abusing his position to get off with women. Must not be a very senior TV twat abusing his position to get off with two women simultaneously. Must not be a very senior TV twat.

Must not be the type to hit on a woman's flatmate.

Must not be the type to dump a woman unceremoniously at Christmas.

Must not be rude to waiters or anyone else working in the service industry.

Must not wear a hat in lieu of a personality.

Must not call for a 'chat' at 2 a.m.

No shaggers. No bigots. No leeches. No egomaniacs. No liars. No narcissists. No time-wasters. NO DICKHEADS!

Otherwise, look forward to hearing from you soooon!

So that was my personal ad, prior to meeting Pete, around 2009. I didn't get much response oddly? Which was particularly annoying because it cost me a fortune per word. OK, so no, I didn't *actually* run this pretty jaded ad. But yes, all that strangely specific information in my pretend personal does largely reference my vast dating experience before Pete. And no, I won't name names.*

(*Unless you buy me a drink.)

*

Now, before I quite rightly big up Pete by comparison to my terrible track record, I want to say two things. First, in addition to the huge amount of crap courting I did, I had some lovely boyfriends and did some very happy dating too (it was largely the couple of years prior to Pete that were particularly exhausting). Second, I don't want to be misconstrued as some smug twat bragging about finally getting herself a 'good man', because like a lot of relationships, things weren't straightforward in those early months between me and Pete either. We met in a bar. We liked each other very much. Then he wasn't sure about me. Subsequently, I wasn't sure about him. We split up briefly. Then we were sure about each other. And we got back together. I know, it's hardly Mills & Boon, but it's *life*. And I have to say it, during those early ardent dates, despite the uncertainty that that sort of intensity throws up, he was very much the breath of fresh air my cynical heart had given up on.

'Do you want kids?' he asked on our third date as we were driving for brunch in a fancy-pants part of Bristol. I was momentarily stunned. Answering this honestly felt dangerous. I could end up feeling like Glenn Close in *Fatal Attraction* with even the slightest whiff of overenthusiasm. All the ghosts of Indifferent Boyfriends Past were whirring before my eyes. I had to answer this carefully. I went with shit humour. 'What for brunch? Not sure I could eat a whole one.'

Pete affectionately tapped my tense knee, probably sweating in the passenger seat. 'Do you though?' he asked, smiling, as we pulled up to our favourite café for a hangover-busting full English. His face was typically open and warm.

Fuck it, I thought, *if he can ask the question, I can answer it*. 'Yes,' I said meeting his eye.

'Me too,' came his quick reply, followed by a swift kiss on my cheek as he unbuckled his seat belt and opened the car door.

It might sound like nothing to some people, but that ridiculously brief exchange was one of the most refreshing I'd ever had over the course of my many dating years. He wasn't saying he wanted kids with me necessarily. He didn't worry that my answer meant I'd immediately start charting my cycle and flipping through the *Big Book of Baby Names*. And over lunch, he and I talked about wanting a *family* specifically, whatever route that took, because between us we had many friends for whom conceiving had been a horribly cruel process. By the end of that lunch, it felt as if we'd established, comfortably and genuinely, that we both wanted the same things – all at Pete's instigation. And while it's frustrating that a woman, particularly in her late thirties as I was then, can be made to feel as if she's holding a bunny over a pot for the briefest mention of babies, I was grateful to Pete for initiating that conversation with such ease.

When I reminded him about it years later, he looked baffled and said: 'How could I not ask? We were in our thirties!'

I wanted to cup his lovely face gently, look tenderly into his eyes and say: 'Pete, my darling, love of my life, you clearly have no fucking idea of what it's like to be a single woman in her thirties…'

Anyway, long story short, two years of living together and falling very much in love, we decided that we were ready to start a family. I came off the pill, very luckily got knocked up with Zain quite quickly and life changed for ever. Our once brunching, lunching, wining, dining relationship now revolved entirely around our beautiful baby boy and competing about who was the more tired (yes, *of course* it was me).

By the time Yasmin came along, life with a toddler and newborn meant date nights were largely on the sofa with a bottle of wine, a sharing bag of Doritos and a film we'd rarely make it through to the end of without one of us falling asleep or Yasmin waking up. However, just because stuff like dating in the traditional sense, plus any sort of personal grooming before a shag, was now a thing of the past, it didn't mean that romance necessarily was too. Romance was just reinvented within the confines of our new lives.

Six piss-easy ways to do romance post-kids

1. Replace swear words with 'love'

When everyday dialogue between you and your other half is like something out of *Pulp Fiction*, thanks to sleep deprivation and the general nerve-battering that comes with having children, it's easy to become a little desensitised.

'Did you make her bottle up?'

'Fuck off.'

'I told you he'd gone off cheese.'

'Shut the fuck up.'

'Can you stop swearing, please?'

'No, I fucking can't.'

Quite rightly, you can each excuse the other's pissiness as sheer fraught fatigue – and to be fair, it's a pretty strong couple who can move past such exchanges with a shrug and a channel-hop. But if you fancy making a gesture out of not effing and jeffing at each other, you could always try replacing your usual four-lettered words with 'love'?

'Love you, you loving love!'

'Love off! And you can forget a love tonight!'

And so on. If, though, sounding like a sweary film with bad dubbing gets a little much, you could always lose the PG-rating after the kids-are-in-bed watershed and let rip with the F word like a couple of motherfuckers…

2. Scoff together at other parents more

This is an easy relationship routine to put into practice and maintain. All that judgement you have for each other's parenting just needs redirecting. As you open your mouth to criticise the spaghetti hoops dished up for the third night in a row, or the amount of

Sudocrem being slapped on your baby's arse – stop and think! Is there someone else whose parenting style you might both enjoy slagging off? The woman round the corner who eats dandelions and has a kid with a name like a shade of Dulux paint? Fair game. Those parents at soft play with the mean kid who twats everyone? Let rip! This is vital, bonding stuff – you're not just enjoying a sneer! You're bitching in a bid to keep your relationship strong, which if you think about it, is all about the kids really.

3. Put out!

No, it's not a reference to sex – it's a cheap gag about putting out the rubbish. A simple effort to sling a bin bag in the black wheelie/ wipe a few surfaces/unwedge the much-hunted for TV remote from between the sofa cushions – or whatever typical household gripe bandied between you – might show more thought than a bunch of begonias ever could. And if shagging is an issue that needs addressing too, let's be honest, you could be more inclined to get off with each other if you're not in a piss about the poo-streaked nappy bags that have been festering on the kitchen floor for days. So remember – get them shit bags shifted and you might get laid. You know, if you both have the energy and there's nothing on TV.

4. Don't shit with the door open

True, it's great that you're very comfortable with each other, and OK, keeping a little 'mystique' in your relationship might be something your nan would advocate. But let's be frank here, seeing poo-strain in your other half's face followed by the stench of human sewage really doesn't set the mood for romance. Excreting in front of your other half, much like eating the contents of your nose or farting and then sniffing the air, given its intrinsic nature to evoke revulsion, has to be a no-no for showing someone you care, surely? Unless, of course you're one of those poo-loving celebrities from many an urban legend – in which case, knock yourself out!

5. Blank each other

Marriage guidance is jam-packed with knackered parents complaining about how loudly the other eats their crisps, or, you know, breathes. But in truth, it's not marital problems they're experiencing, it's just a touch of cabin fever. It's unsurprising really, given that leaving the house with kids is so protracted that plans are often abandoned and consequently, by witching hour, everyone is losing their shit like contestants on *Big Brother*. It's not expensive counselling you need, or to ram whole packets of crisps down your other half's throat in a bid to secure a bit of peace. You just need to sit in separate rooms happily blanking each other for a while. For a lifetime, maybe. Sure, you'll still hate each other, but then at least you can go on game shows together, and get a round of applause from the studio audience for not getting divorced over the course of fifty-odd years.

6. Skin up!

Enjoyed a little reefer before having kids? Maybe you frequented the odd illegal rave together prior to a life full of 'Nellie the Elephant'? Or perhaps a quick fumble in a public place was more your thing? Whatever your favourite cheeky pastime pre-parent days, you could benefit from revisiting those dark, dirty, delicious days. Slumping next to each other, gawking at your respective phones and swapping the odd bit of information about unpaid bills and what time the Tesco delivery is due can become all too familiar when kids drain you of your last drop of energy. So crack open the Rizla, stick on a Prodigy CD and enjoy a little under-the-sweater by an open window – because you're not just parents. You are a couple of lovely freaks with some weird shit in common.

Again, I'd like to assure you that I am not a spliff head. These references are for comic purposes only, I *swear*. And I'd just like to reiterate the humorous tone and intention of this piece, in case it's misconstrued as it was by one commenter, when a (heavily subbed) version of this was commissioned for a national newspaper. Apparently, the commenter was very concerned that I was not appropriately qualified for dishing out relationship advice. Wow. What gave me away…?

When Pete met Papa…

Anyway, back to Pete and how I'm always right. Well, actually, not according to Papa. Whenever we bicker, he'll always take Pete's side. Because Papa adores Pete. 'You mustn't bully, Pete,' he'll scold. 'Pete is a good boy!' And Pete will give me a gloating look as if to say, *Ha! You got done!* But the truth is, you know your dad probably prefers your other half to you when you arrive at your dad's and his first question, as he looks over your shoulder, is: 'Where's Pete?'

Papa is the same with my lovely brother-in-law and I remember my sister saying, with so much pride, that the bond between them was instant when she first took him home to meet Papa. I could sense how emotional that must have been; how defining it must have felt. And I had exactly the same sentiments. Pete was the first boyfriend I'd ever taken to meet Papa and having the two men I loved most in the world meet was a huge deal. Papa is at the heart of everything in our lives and introducing someone special to my dad was a declaration – one that made me nervous in case that honour was lost on the recipient. But seeing Pete chuckle appreciatively at Papa's bad jokes, and have so much affection for my dear dad within minutes of meeting him, blew me away. Equally, observing Papa's delicious home-made curry spread, the ironed shirt he was wearing especially for the occasion and the way he enjoyed Pete's appreciative chuckles bowled me over. Papa had welcomed Pete into the family.

Since then, Papa and Pete have grown so fond of each other, it's a very sweet sight to behold. The pair have now even assumed a fairly regular weekly routine. Papa brandishes at Pete his phone, radio, TV remote and countless other gadgets for repair, then Pete sets about fixing them while Papa plants a kiss on the top of his head and calls him a good boy for the ten thousandth time. He then wags a jokey warning finger at me as if the completion of these 'Papa projects' are good-deed down payments against Pete being 'picked on'.

'I don't pick on you,' I protested recently as we were driving home from Papa's. 'I just end up having to nag a lot – generally about the same things – because you don't listen!'

'Well, we at least agree that you nag me a lot – Papa clearly thinks so too!' Pete gave a wry smile.

After much slightly tetchy and defensive discussion, we agreed since having kids that our relationship has seen me griping far more at him than the other way around. Maybe this sounds familiar?

So, at my request, he wrote a list of the most consistent earbashes he's been on the receiving end of since becoming a dad. I have written my defence for each underneath. I hope you'll take my side.

Some earbashings Pete (quite rightly) receives on a regular basis

When I pass on any advice about motherhood from my mum

I want to say first and foremost, I love Pete's mum very much and she has *never* been one for unsolicited parenting advice. But Pete did enjoy a little 'My mum never did that' and 'I'll ask my mum', particularly on the back of me pondering on some child-related health or milestone matter when Zain and Yasmin were babies.

It was hugely annoying. Mainly because Pete would then live and die by that advice. I could quote reams of well-reasoned argument from critically acclaimed books written by Nobel Prize-winning scholars. I could present a PowerPoint presentation full of comprehensive, evidence-based facts and illustrative pie charts. I could even fly the Director General of the World Health Organization, Dr Tedros Adhanom Ghebreyesus, over from Geneva to Bristol, have him stand in our kitchen, articulate the extensive fieldwork he's completed on the matter in hand, accompanied by in-the-flesh case studies and world-renowned academics with loads of letters after their names. And still Pete would mutter: 'Well, it's just that my mum said…'

When I let you know I've done some housework

As I've mentioned, Pete is partial to letting me know he's done a household chore, which I might do (arguably more frequently) without the big announcement. He also likes to repeat this broadcast just to make sure I'm fully aware:

'I emptied the bin, by the way.'

'The bin's been emptied, just so you know.'

'Did I mention I've emptied the bin?'

By the third reference, I'm generally aware I haven't shown sufficient gratitude for the completion of the household chore. So now I have two responses:

'I've sent out the press release, there's a photoshoot at midday and Krishnan Guru-Murthy wants to interview you for *Channel 4 News* by the bin. He asked if you'd be happy walking him through how you emptied the bin…?'

Or (hours after the third announcement has gone out):

'Remind me, did you say you'd emptied the bin – or hadn't emptied the bin?'

When I simply rest a new roll of toilet paper on the empty cardboard tube sitting in the toilet-roll holder

How hard is it? SERIOUSLY? One uses loo. One observes toilet roll is now empty. One takes new toilet roll. One replaces cardboard inner with new roll. One puts the empty in the recycling. THE END! But apparently this only works if 'one' is not Pete! I'll never understand what goes through his mind. He knows I will never be some long-suffering wife in a 1970s sitcom, who rolls her eyes, replaces the loo roll (while also putting the toilet seat down), and then sighs with a chuckle: 'Men! Gah!' He knows he'll be getting an earbashing and correcting that oversight himself! There should be some sort of course, a bit like dog training, where such people (note I didn't say men – I don't want Fathers 4 Justice trolling me) can be educated in how to do the following:

- Fully change a loo roll.
- Retrieve dirty undergarments from the floor and place them in the laundry basket.
- Make toast without leaving a layer of crumb-grit over every available surface.
- Put shoes on the shoe rack and not in the vague vicinity of the shoe rack.
- Use stairs for ascending and descending, and not as a storage facility.
- Match Tupperware containers with their lids when empty-ing the dishwasher, so they are not rendered useless and end up sitting in a cupboard with several hundred other bits of lidless containers.

- Not pack down waste matter in the bin as a means of not emptying it, so the regular emptier of the bin is then left covered in bin juice when the liner splits because it can't bear the burden of its supressed contents.

(Yes, that bin is totally a metaphor for our relationship.)

When I buy toys for the kids that I like playing with as well

Currently sitting in our hallway is a remote-controlled truck. It's about the size of a Yorkshire Terrier and is very much Pete's pet. It cost about (this bit chokes me a little) £150. Yes, you read that right. It was allegedly bought as a joint present for Zain and Yasmin. Neither barely get a look-in.

Similarly, I find boxes of Lego stashed in corners of the house the way addicts hide their drug of choice. We've emptied IKEA of all its storage items and we now have units full of toys the kids no longer play with, but Pete can't bear to part with – because he's a FRICKIN' CHILD! OK, I realise that's a little mean, but please bear in mind, my home has so many elaborate Lego displays, Star Wars paraphernalia and superhero figures, all passing as 'decor', it's like living with Will Ferrell in *Elf*.

When I go just 1 mph over the speed limit with the kids in the car

OK, so yes, I'm a little neurotic and will scream 'SLOW DOWN' on occasions when Pete is not even speeding (you don't *have* to go up to the speed limit, right?) But since becoming a mum, I can't deny it, I torture myself with anxiety in the car. I'll ask the kids approximately fifteen times if they're strapped in, even if I've belted them in myself. I'll wince at the sight of an oncoming lorry or bus. And with the tiniest bit of difficult driving to contend with,

I close my eyes dramatically, clutch the car-door armrest with the grip of a woodworking vice and persistently push my foot down on an imaginary brake (as a passenger, I hasten to add, not on one of the rare occasions I'm actually driving). So, fine, it's true, I'm not entirely reasonable as a passenger with the kids in the car. Alright, I'm a nightmare. But the minute I'm Prime Minister (it'll happen), I'm halving the speed limit across the entire country and making milk floats the mandatory mode of transportation for everyone.

When I compare myself favourably to other
'do-nothing' dads

You might know a few of these yourself? The ones with 'man caves'. The ones who consider themselves 'babysitting' when looking after their offspring. The ones who couldn't possibly get up with the baby in the night because they have a job to go to during the day (while raising a human 24-7, with no lunch breaks, no leisurely pees and no lovely unrushed coffees is clearly one of those 'toy' jobs rich Sloanes have to pass the time of day). Well, Pete has thankfully never been one of those ridiculous relics. He's loved being a parent and has been a bloody brilliant one at that.

However, when I'd see his eyes light up as some bloke bragged about dodging nappy changes or said he just 'couldn't function' without six hours of continuous sleep, I knew he was storing it all up, filing it in a mental cabinet labelled 'Do-Nothing Dads to Reference When Next Nagged'. 'Can you imagine,' he'd say smugly afterwards, 'if I hid in a man cave and never changed a shitty nappy! You'd go off on one!' And I'd point out, as I did every time: 'All true, Peter, but why do you assume to compare yourself with the cave-dwelling dick in that scenario? WHY NOT COMPARE YOURSELF LESS FAVOURABLY WITH THE "DO-EVERYTHING" MUM? KNOBBER!'

*

I jest, of course. Pete is not a knobber. Yes, he can be quite slovenly. OK, I hate his driving. And true, I live in a home filled with so much Pete-purchased plastic tat, I wouldn't be able to look Greta Thunberg in the eye were I to meet her. (Bear with me, with I'm going somewhere with this.) But he's beyond brilliant as a husband and dad. As I've been writing this book, largely over the summer holidays, he's been looking after the kids, cooking for us all, cleaning – well, OK, not cleaning, but tending to everything Zain and Yasmin need so I'm not disturbed. If they ask him to play a game or read something with them, he never refuses – and that's no exaggeration. He's loving, kind, doting, supportive and could never be a cave-dwelling dick. He's far too smart to move in such sad provincial circles.

It's true, I'm still the one between us badgered via WhatsApp groups or passive-aggressive requests at the school gates to take part in bake sales and assist on class trips (because apparently only a person with a vagina is capable of anything vaguely domestic or nurturing). But Pete will happily host playdates, do the school run, check their homework and many other school-related activities a mum often finds herself in sole charge of. And I know regarding myself as 'lucky' is not how things should be (after all, we both work and are both Zain and Yasmin's parents), but I have encountered enough cave-dwelling dicks to know that, actually, I am fortunate. In fact, from the minute Pete casually asked me on that third date if I wanted kids, he was in a class of his own.

Having a dad as exceptional as mine, particularly when it comes to parenting with that level of wholehearted nonconformity, meant that whoever I had kids with, as I always hoped to, had some pretty big Crocs to fill. But Pete so does. If I had run my fake personal ad, he would have exceeded all expectations. He'd have probably even had the guts to apply because, fortunately for me, he likes a gobby, forthright woman. He has an abundance of patience as I'm actually quite hard to live with (I know, it's a shock, right?). He can make me cackle when I'm in the biggest of pisses with him. He laughs at (most of) my jokes. His kindness is etched all over his lovely face. He gives heart-warming, restorative hugs. He tells me and the kids that he loves us every day. He makes those years of dire dating prior to meeting him all entirely worthwhile. He is, as we say in Bristol, just lush.

So, finally, in 2019, after ten years, three homes and two kids… reader, I married him. Because Papa's right, Pete is a good boy.

CHAPTER EIGHT

New Mum on the Piss

'You know, Zeena, it won't make you cool or like a big lady…'

If you're having trouble passing a pub or bar doorway without sniffing the air, gulping in its yeasty, musty essence, and longing to lose a few hours amid its reclaimed-wood decor, it could be that you're ready for your first night out away from the baby. It's a monumental milestone for any mum. It's like regaining a little of your pre-baby self and can feel totally liberating. But, of course, being a mum now means your social life is inevitably not quite the same. Getting rat-arsed is dangerously easy for starters, as your threshold for alcohol consumption is not and will never be the same. Your outfit choices are likely to be of the elasticated-waist variety. And of course, sorting the night out itself will take the planning skills of a military defence strategist.

Here's a little pre- and post-kids comparison to clarify how drastically different a night out was for twenty-something childfree me, and me after having Zain…

Pre-kids me: 'Tonight? A bar? Then a house party, approximately thirty miles across town, after? Sure! I'll meet you in the pub in twenty!'
Post-kids me: 'A few sensible glasses of wine in the nice gastro pub with comfy seating and no young people whatsoever? Sounds lovely! How does Friday fifteenth, in about two years' time suit?'

Pre-kids me: 'What you wearing tonight? I'm thinking a titchy top, with no bra, and a skirt that used to be my hairband?'

Post-kids me: [Almost opens vein in H&M amid noisy, foetus-aged shoppers, before deciding posset-smeared maternity shirt already wearing will do.]

Pre-kids me: [Applies three different kinds of eyeshadow, seventeen layers of mascara, concealer, foundation, lipliner, lipstick, some sort of shimmery face highlighter thing, brow shaper that doesn't actually do much and enough black eyeliner to rival Siouxsie and the Banshees circa 1984.]

Post-kids me: [Applies nipple cream as gloss to lips and runs nit comb through hair.]

Pre-kids me: [checking titchy handbag] 'Right, so I've got keys, money, cash card, fags, lighter, make-up for reapplication, taxi numbers and tissues in case latest break-up gets the better of me – again. Yep, I'm all set!'

Post-kids me: [Picks up ginormous, one-and-only hand-cum-changing bag crammed with teethers, wipes, bum cream, thirty-six different types of snacks and massive mum purse housing several years' worth of receipts and out-of-date membership cards to absolutely everything.]

Pre-kids me: [Arrives at bar half an hour late, orders a pint of lager, a shot to 'catch up' and a packet of cheese and onion to line dangerously empty tummy.]

Post-kids me: 'Can I get the Pinot Noir please? I'll have a small please. No, a medium. No wait, I'll have a large. Oh, go on, I'll get the bottle. Be cheaper in the long run…'

Pre-kids me: 'Oh, CHOOOON! Ask Phil the fit barman to turn it up!'

Post-kids me: 'Sorry to trouble you, would you mind awfully turning the music down? It's just that we're trying to have a nice chat about childcare and catchment areas.'

Pre-kids me: 'Oh my God, is it 10.50? Who fancies a seventh drink before they call time? Oi! Camel Mouth! Another beer?'

Post-kids me: 'Oh my God, is it 9.30? I better think about heading soon. I feel quite pissed. How much have I had? Really? Just the two?'

Pre-kids me: 'Right, taxi's here! Carla! Put Phil down! Jo! Step away from the WKD! Jules! Stop gurning! Complete-and-utter-stranger's house party – here we come!'

Post-kids me: 'I think thash my cab? Ish he shtopping? Yezzit is my cab! Oh, I love you guys! Let's do it again tomorrow, pleeeeeeash? Do I look drunk, Lou? You'd tell me, right? I loves you, Lou. Have I really jussh had the two? How about my teeth, Lou? Are they black, Lou?' [Bares black teeth like Jack Nicholson at poor Lou.]

The next morning...

Pre-kids me: 'God, I can't believe I went to bed at 5.30 this morning! What was his name again? He seemed nice. Anyway, definitely a telly and takeaway on the sofa kinda day! Right after I leisurely finish my eggs benedict and lovely quiet read of the papers...'

Post-kids me: 'God, I can't believe I was up with the baby at 5.30 this morning! Did I really say I'd go to the zoo today? Fuuuuck. OK, I'll just change his shitty nappy, throw up a bit more, lock myself in the bathroom for a solid fifteen minutes of some remorseful self-loathing, and then I'll be ready to go.'

Of course, a lot of this is embellished before you judge pre-kids me too harshly; I was never posh enough to breakfast on eggs benedict in my twenties...

If you're feeling ready for a night on the razz, first and foremost, might I suggest you stock up on the painkillers? Get the heavy-duty stuff because hangovers when you have children are a whole new world of pain. Might I also suggest that you do your first night of boozing with fellow mums, because a) it will be an equal playing field when it comes to low levels of alcohol tolerance, and b) you'll be more readily forgiven for repeatedly texting home to check in, and brandishing 1,000 phone photos of your baby throughout the evening. I don't want to be misconstrued, however, as suggesting that people without children are no longer good booze buddies (no one should want to be that mum moron who can't make sense of childfree women and says narcissistic guff like, 'You don't know what love is until you have kids'). My latter suggestion is based solely on easing you into your first night on the sauce as a mum, with your emotions and liver my primary concern.

Once you have a few mum piss-ups under your belt, you'll start to become, as I soon did, familiar with the many mums-on-the-lash types we mothers often inadvertently assume, in the process of both organising and executing a night out…

Which type of mum-on-the-piss are you?

Planning a night on the razz with a mum friend or two soon? Anticipating the usual last-minute text blowing you out because of some kid-related reason? Bracing yourself for the mate drunk before she's finished straightening her hair, because she's forgotten that fuck-all sleep and alcohol are not great mixers? Sound all too familiar? Perhaps because that flaky, knackered, wankered friend is YOU!

Poor-Listener Mum Friend

Conversations with this mum-type during a daytime meet-up often feel like a bad signal connection on a mobile, thanks to her unrelenting kids and sleep-deprived memory. 'I am listening,' she'll insist as she puts a wash on, shouts at her scrapping offspring and then wanders upstairs to bleach the loo. 'Go on,' she'll call from over the banister clutching a poo-speckled loo brush, 'I'm still listening.' But she so isn't – because with or without her kids around, habitual multi-tasking at 1,000 mph has given her an attention span not dissimilar to a frenzied toddler. So if you're booking a boozy bender with a poor-listening mum friend be prepared to repeat yourself – a lot. Better still, get bladdered and then you can talk at each other bombastically and repetitively, as pissed people tend to do, and it won't matter quite so much.

Expect this text before a night out with her: *What time are we meeting again? Where are we meeting? Who are we meeting? Are we eating? Worra-ma-like! LOL! X!*

Stage-School Mum Friend

This mum has big plans for her children. RADA, Sylvia Young, Italia Conti – they won't know what's hit them when her kids pas de bourrée across the stage, jazz hands aloft. Until that day, it is generally unsuspecting house guests she thrusts a poor reluctant child in front of, demanding they observe a song or dance or both. Of course, it all then gets a bit awkward when her kid stands there mute for several minutes as Stage-School Mum mutters apologetically, 'I don't understand it, he was doing it earlier…' Expect a similar level of neediness on a night out with her because, in the absence of a child to wield, her phone will be thrust in your face, full of endless living-room performances for you to coo over.

Expect this text before a night out with her: *Remind me to show you the video of Tabby singing all nine verses of 'Let It Go'. OMG, you will die! Sooo cute. Her key worker at nursery said she is so much like Britney before the breakdown, it's unbelievable… L8rs!*

Flaky Mum Friend

Virtually everyone has a flaky mum friend. Lunches are cancelled last minute, texts go unanswered and postponed catch-ups are rarely rescheduled. Truth be told, a friendship with her requires a lot of patience and persistence as she rattles off child-related excuse after excuse. But trust that one day – perhaps when a midlife crisis strikes and she rocks up at your house in a pair of leather trousers, a bifta dangling from her lip and her hand on the arse of a passing pizza boy she's pulled – she will reward that perseverance with more debauchery than you can shake a glow stick at. In the meantime, however, you should probably best prepare to party without her.

Expect this text before a night out with her (minutes before you're due to meet up): *Hi hun, so sorry but I'm not going to be able to make it. Jonah sneezed three times – in a row – and I'm really worried he's got pneumonia. GUTTED to miss you for the seventeenth time, obvs. Soz hun xxxx*

Hammered-by-9 p.m. Mum Friend

Unlike Flaky, this mum friend *never* misses a catch-up or night out – especially if there's booze involved. An evening with her will regularly see absinthe downed, waiters goosed, mum-moves busted – it's never dull. It's all good fun until she's so twatted she can barely walk and then suddenly you're the friend hunting for her bag/holding her hair/placating a very angry bouncer. She does it every time. In her excitement to be away from her children, she peaks far too soon, forgetting her stamina has been seriously depleted from the exertion of pushing babies out of her vagina and then having to raise them. As she vows, in between sobbing and chundering, never to do this again, smile sweetly and pretend you believe her.

Expect this text before a night out with her: *Yo beeeyatch! Shall I get the cab to swing by Oddbins on the way over to yours? Thought we could swig a few Breezers before we hit The Oak? Truth be told, I've had a few already making tea… Shhh! Def not pis$ed th8ugh honesT x*

Baby-Bore Mum Friend

It's rare to get Baby-Bore Mum Friend out for a night, because for her, a lovely evening is tucked up with a copy of *Baby-led Weaning*, or tutting angrily in front of *Supernanny*. If you do manage to entice her out, you should probably brace yourself for a barrage of baby theories and updates on her own kid's development. Nod in all the right places and bristle angrily on her behalf when she relays how 'outrageous' the health visitor was when she very casually informed her that her baby was slightly above the fiftieth percentile.

Expect this text before a night out with her: *Just to warn you, I might be a little late tonight because Jocasta has terrible separation anxiety. According to* What to Expect, *her cortisol levels are probably higher because of her primitive instincts that I will abandon her in the wild and leave her to be devoured by a man-eating animal. Anyway, I'll tell you all about it when I see you! Ciao!*

Over-Sharer Mum Friend

The carnage that accompanies becoming a mum was a shock to the system for this friend-type, and as a result, she spends a lot of time audibly reeling from the various bodily fluid and gunk she regularly deals with. 'Does this look like mastitis to you?' she'll ask as she waps out a bap in Starbucks. 'You could bungee jump with that bogie,' she'll muse, holding up the stretchy lime green matter she's just extracted from her baby's nostril. Presume to feel yet more bilious on an evening jaunt because those social skills are well and truly shot, regardless of the adult environment, people around her attempting to consume food and drink, and the dry heaving that follows virtually everything she says.

Expect this text before a night out with her: *Running a bit late – sorry! Had to deal with a massive shit! Honestly, you've never seen anything like it – was like a jar of piccalilli had exploded into every imaginable crevice! Bleurgh! My bowels have definitely not been the same since having kids… TMI?! Probably! Bye! Xx*

Brings-Her-Kids Mum Friend

A bit like a trendy supply teacher, this mum believes you get the best out of kids if you treat them like adults. Consequently, an invitation to a dinner party at her house will generally entail a five-year-old sitting at the head of the table conversing in French with her stuffed Babar the Elephant, and an overtired three-year-old, still up at 10 p.m., screaming, 'I HATE couscous and I hate YOU!' You should fully anticipate beholding a similar scene if you are foolish enough to arrange an evening in a public place with her.

Expect this text before a night out with her: *Hi darling, you don't mind if I bring India and Tilly with me, do you? Duncan and I are really keen to respect them as individuals and not impose restrictive routines that might impact negatively on their cognitive development. They're fabulous company though, and Tilly has some wonderful insight she wants to share with you about utopian socialism…*

Can't-Shake-Her-Off Mum Friend

OK, her time-keeping is pretty tardy, frequently blustering in late for lunches with a child on each hip and the usual someone-shat-everywhere explanations. True, she sends your birthday present generally three weeks after the actual date. And yes, she has a terrible tendency to cry off from two in every three planned nights out. But try as you may, you can't shake this mum-mate off. She will never be completely off the radar because, much like those very profound Spice Girls, she believes friendship never ends. Even when you wish she'd zigga zig-ah off, she'll be there, slamming her body down, winding it all around… You know, *eventually…*

Expect this text before a night out with her: *Cannot WAIT to see you! Let's do shots! And cocktails! And go dancing! And get off with boys! Oh no, wait – better not do that… LMFAO! Do you remember that time you shagged that lad behind the Humanities block? Didn't he give you an "A" for your coursework in the end?! Anyway, see you later! LOVE YOU.*

I'm obviously pretty much all of these types and, often, all on the same night out (except Brings-Her-Kids Mum because that shit is just really annoying).

Actually, these days, I rarely go out. I generally don't see the point of leaving home when I have a rack full of wine and Netflix (aside from the wine, Papa would be proud). With a childhood of mainly yearning for more social life, I often wonder if my teenage self would be appalled to see all the freedom I waste.

When I was about seventeen, I tried explaining to a friend, on the back of my dad refusing to let me join her and some other friends for a night of clubbing, that Papa's Indian-Muslim background very much shaped his strictness.

She looked bemused: 'But he doesn't really practise Islam?'

I told her that it wasn't necessarily about him being a practising Muslim, but it was more a cultural thing.

'So if my mum says I'm not allowed out, is that cultural?' she asked defensively.

'No,' I said, trying hard not to roll my eyes. 'It's not.'

I attempted again to present things in a way she might understand but eventually gave up when I could see it was pointless. Her very British, bohemian middle-class background was too entrenched for her to relate to my upbringing. It's funny, but friends with strict foreign parents, particularly those of South Asian descent, rarely needed this sort of explanation.

To illustrate just how stringent Papa could be when it came to allowing me out, this is how a conversation in my early teens would often go, as I'd attempt to seek permission to go out after 7 p.m.:

Me: 'Dad, can I go—'
Papa: 'NO!'
Me: 'But you don't even—'
Papa: 'NO!'
Me: 'Why—'
Papa: 'NO!'

He started to relent a little more as I progressed further into secondary school and instead of a flat 'No', I was allowed out, but with a strict time limit (and I should point out that back then in the 1980s, safety concerns weren't what they are now, when Papa's overprotection might seem more routine). This is how a conversation would often go when I then had to negotiate a curfew:

Me: 'Can I stay out until eleven?'
Papa: 'What? NO!'
Me: 'What time do I have to be home then?'
Papa: 'Eight thirty.'
Me: 'What? NO WAY! That's SO embarrassing. It's hardly worth me going out!'
Papa: 'GOOD! Don't go out then!'
Me: 'Ten thirty?'
Papa: 'What? NO!'
Me: 'What time then? And don't say eight thirty.'
Papa: 'OK, nine. But that's it.'
Me [now on the brink of tears]: 'No, pleeeease don't make me come home at nine.'
Papa: 'OK, nine thirty. BUT THAT IS IT, I MEAN IT, DON'T NAG ANY MORE! AND NOT A MINUTE LATER!'

The negotiation would continue in vain, but 9.30 p.m. was the bottom line, until I was about fifteen and allowed out until 10 p.m. This was a big deal and at least elevated me to the circles of the kids with strict parents of normal proportions. (And again, I must credit my big sister for paving the way for me and my brother, with her Rob Roy-like quest for fairer teenage freedom.) However, if we'd dared to be more than five minutes late, we risked the monumentally embarrassing scene, such as follows:

[Me and a group of friends hanging around the playing fields, one summer night at approximately 10.05 p.m.]
Friend 1: 'Er, Zee, is that your dad?'
Boy I fancied: 'He don't look happy!'
Friend 2: 'Ooh, Zee, you're getting DONE!'
[Me, silently praying they're wrong, turning my head slowly round to see the unmistakable bald head and frowning face of Papa striding through the goal posts of the fields]
Papa [his voice booming across the park]: 'ZEEEENAAAA! COME HOME NOOOOW!'
Me [legging it towards Papa before he could reach us and the real mortification would commence]: 'I was just coming home! Oh, my God, you're so embarrassing!'

I love Papa very much, as you know, but seriously, that is kryptonite to a teenager, right? I can still feel the humiliation in my hot cheeks recalling my friends and the boy I fancied laughing (I mean you would, to be fair), as I ran like Zola Budd across that field in an attempt to salvage any dignity there was left. I was seething with resentment and I imagine my diary got a right mouthful about Papa that night...

Papa became far less strict once I started my A levels, and almost overnight (doffs cap at trailblazing big sister), I was allowed to go out with friends into Bristol and get the last bus home at 11.20 p.m.! Still though, Papa would call after me as I'd clatter off to catch the 354 into town: 'No drinking! I don't like it! It won't make you cool or like a big lady!'

Of course, being a bored teenager growing up in suburbia, I did drink, and as a typical arrogant arsehole of a teen, I always presumed Papa was just unaware. I'd plucked up the courage to tell him I was a smoker when I was about seventeen, and while he grimaced and told me he didn't approve, he reluctantly accepted it. But it never occurred to me to confess to boozing, even at the legal age of eighteen, especially given his Muslim background, being teetotal his whole life and expressing distinct disapproval of it. So, underestimating Papa, like the fool I was, I was sure he believed I spent evenings out with friends quaffing squash all night. But then, one evening, while out in a Bristol bar with my favourite friend Carla, I was caught Red Stripe-handed and there was nowhere to hide…

It was a Saturday night, and Carla and I had not long sat down, ready to tuck into our lovely lagers and shoot the breeze about crushes and coursework. I glanced around to survey the artsy crowd and was feeling particularly smug about my studenty surroundings and impending happy higher education days. With a freshly lit Silk Cult, I was about to enjoy my first sip of lager, when I spotted through the dense crowd a familiar pair of unfashionably flared, navy nylon men's trousers, complete with sharp crease. This was not the typical preferred attire of the youthful clientele we were amid, and I froze mid sip, scanning slowly up the wearer of the navy nylon trousers.

'That bloke looks like my dad,' I said to Carla, half laughing. My face suddenly fell. 'Shit! That *is* my dad!'

Carla's face also fell. We both looked as if we'd been summoned to the headmaster's office. Papa was with his friend Hassan, visiting from London, also a South African-Indian, but very much an atheist and, also, occasional drinker of alcohol. Hassan smiled and waved as they were approaching. Papa was frowning – but as he got closer, I could see it was a comical scowl. It definitely wasn't the frown from the playing fields looming towards me.

As Papa and Hassan joined us at the table, Hassan explained that he'd asked my dad where I'd headed to for the evening and suggested they join us, as he fancied a beer too. I nodded, half taking in what Hassan was saying. My eyes were still wide and veering between the lager on the table in front of me and Papa standing over me to my right.

'What's this?' Papa pointed at my beer. Before I could answer, he turned to Carla giving her his precursor-to-a-piss-take smile: 'It's non-alcoholic, isn't it, Carla?'

Carla laughed and I felt myself exhale for the first time since spotting the navy nylon trousers in the crowd.

I still hadn't said anything and was about to get up to source chairs for Papa and Hassan, when Papa looked at me and said: 'What is it you're drinking? I'll get the same again.' I was gob-smacked! I stammered out the drinks order for Carla and me and watched in shock as he walked up to the bar, simultaneously reaching for his wallet in his shirt pocket.

When he returned and put the drinks down in front of us, he looked at me with his comical scowl again, and said: 'But I don't like it, Zee.' And that was it! The pretence that I was drinking Diet Coke when I went to pubs and bars was over! It was as if Papa had called time on the charade out of sheer weariness of being wildly underestimated.

I asked Papa recently if he felt he had been strict with us while we were growing up. He shrugged. 'Probably. But I just did what I thought was right for you all. And, you know, Zeena, when I was growing up in South Africa, I was only allowed out once a week to a film matinee in the school hall! Your grandfather was very conservative. We all had to be home by Maghrib prayers and if we were late, he'd be very cross. There'd be no cinema that week! And if you'd dare protest, you could lose next week's cinema trip! You all had it very easy compared to me and my brothers and sisters.

'You know, Zee, Papa even used to come looking for me if I was out after Maghrib. I'd be standing outside a friend's house, just chatting, and he'd come find me to order me home! My friends used to tease me! It was very embarrassing. Can you imagine?'

I smiled at his sweet, guileless question. Maybe history really does repeat itself and I should make my peace with mortifying Zain and Yasmin in front of their friends now?

'No, Dad,' I replied. 'I can't imagine.'

CHAPTER NINE

Food *is* Love

'You know, Zeena, you must eat – everything I have in the house.'

OK, first, let me stress this again. I breastfed both my children, pretty much exclusively, for seven and eight months respectively. So I am really, really not 'anti-breastfeeding', or getting paid a shitload of money by Aptamil to flog formula. I found it hard at the beginning. But then it got easier. I began to love breastfeeding and, soon after, would look forward to those feeds with both my kids. Pete and I decided to move on to formula around the time I was going back to work. I found it almost as hard to stop breast-feeding, but ultimately was very comfortable with the decision. (A slightly curt, really condensed version of my breastfeeding journey for you there.)

But I can't deny it, when it comes to conversations around breastfeeding, there's a sanctimonious, privileged rhetoric, particularly over recent years, that frequently gets on my tits, lactating and otherwise. A (male) TV chef suggested on a radio show that more new mums should be breastfeeding because it was 'easy' and 'convenient'. A top model felt compelled to say in a magazine interview that new mothers should be forced by 'worldwide law' to breastfeed for at least six months. An actress and presenter stated matter-of-factly, during a daytime chat show, that she thought many women didn't breastfeed because they were just plain 'lazy' (presumably too worried about Ofcom to use the word 'chavvy'). And of course, I encountered enough opinion from many a woman in a Birkenstock during both maternity leaves to feel, as an *exclusively breastfeeding mother* (just using italics to really hammer home the point I'm not masking some aggressive bottle-feeding agenda) that there was a snobbery to that huffy world.

Of course, there are many weird breastfeeding shamers out there, as I've experienced, who could do with being dragged by the scruff of their gammony necks into the new millennium. But, in our society, I feel there is a distinct, middle-class loftiness when it comes to that style of breastfeeding advocacy and it irks me. It's a bit like the shame Papa encountered back in the 1980s for his ready-meal frozen fare in Bejam; somehow such impoverished, malnourished mortals are letting the human race down and deserve to be publicly flogged, like the deprived peasants they are.

I would never dream, of course, to dispute cold, hard, medical fact. Breast milk contains antibodies that help your baby fight off viruses and bacteria, plus lowers your baby's risk of having asthma or allergies. Research has shown that babies who are breastfed exclusively for the first six months have fewer ear infections, respiratory illnesses and bouts of diarrhoea. Breastfeeding mums reportedly also reduce their chances of breast cancer by around 50 per cent. Formula cannot do any of this. Most of us, from the minute we're pregnant, are consistently absorbing the very clear, well-elaborated message 'breast is best' with every prenatal appointment we attend. So when physical and emotional reasons in particular are at the heart of a woman's reasons for not breastfeeding, it can be utterly devastating.

I've witnessed friends feel as if they've failed their child, and sheepishly overexplain to a stranger why breastfeeding didn't work out for them. I've seen the tears shed because of the miserable mastitis which resulted in more blood than milk, or the tongue tie that made breastfeeding pretty much impossible. I've had heart-to-hearts where the depression had become unbearable and formula feeding was a means of alleviating that darkness as a friend salvaged slightly more sleep. I've observed the self-conscious discomfort around a conversation as a few mums shared their happy experiences of when the latch finally 'clicked'. It's too sad. Because, however stigmatised I might have felt as a breastfeeding mum in public, it was nothing compared to this sort of pain.

I was lucky. I had an *amazing* midwifery team with both my two, and when reflux shot everything to shit, and exclusive, dairy-and-soya-free breastfeeding was the only option I had to help soothe my babies' regurgitating bellies, they were with me every step of the engorged-boobed, sore-nippled way. As many mothers know, 'fed is best' is a well-worn phrase, but I'm going to supplement that with 'fed and supported is best'. Not a particularly catchy slogan, I concede; just quite simply the boring truth. When it comes to how we feed our kids, all mothers need empathetic support, not demeaning judgement slapped in their faces.

I found the world of weaning to have a similar virtuous vibe to it. Again, like the age-old bottle versus breast wrangle, there appears to be mainly two camps – traditional and baby-led weaning – with some of those in the latter clique, in my experience, tending to be more righteous in their views. Baby-led, or BLW as it's often abbreviated to in social-media circles, is about presenting foods in largely sliced form (such as soft sticks of fruit and boiled or steamed vegetables) for the baby to grab hold of and feed themselves, as opposed to spoon-feeding a baby puree. The idea is that a child is encouraged to be more independent and get used to different textures as soon as they're of official weaning age, with different stage-appropriate foods as they progress. There is also belief that a child is less likely to be a fussy eater as a result of baby-led weaning. While I can't quote evidence to support the rationale behind any of this, it all sounds pretty reasonable, right? Until you browse the internet, and BLW can suddenly feel like a cult…

Below is a sample of responses I found in a few online forums to various women innocuously looking for top tips on how to introduce BLW to their babies, having already dabbled with a little puree (one mum even brave enough to admit she'd used a jar). Brace yourself; you might experience a little altitude sickness from all the moral high ground you are about to encounter…

- *'Baby-led weaning does not involve purees/mashing/blending or any carer-led spoon-feeding! I don't have any information about graduating from puree to baby-led, because I didn't do that.'*
- *'I didn't go down the puree route at all… If it were me, I'd drop the baby rice and purees pronto and get him on to real food ASAP. Even if it meant he ate nothing at all for the next few weeks.'*
- *'You simply give baby some food and they will feed themselves. It's that simple. Do they 'need' to eat puree??? Absolutely not. Purees were a strange invention for force-feeding infants.'*
- *'Baby-led weaning means no parent-assisted foods, so in other words if the child can't get the food to their mouth without help they are not yet ready for it. They don't need to eat pureed stuff at all! Purees are completely unnecessary.'*
- *'What's your concern? Because you might have a little more to clean up? Wow, how lazy!'*
- *'The whole purpose of baby-led weaning is allowing the baby to self-feed. You cannot self-feed with commercially prepared pureed food.'*

- '[My children] *were having things like toast soldiers with soya butter, avocado, banana and steamed squash, all at six months. None of my children were ever fed from a jar or a pouch. That's not BLW and there is no nutrition in those things.'*
- *'Since you've already been feeding your baby commercially prepared infant food, you are currently doing parent-led weaning.'* [No additional information offered.]

It's off its head, isn't it? Such angry, almost conspiracy-like theories around spoon-feeding – and even a suggestion that NO food is better than 'force-feeding' puree? It feels quasi-religious: thou shalt NEVER deviate from the sacred BLW text, because if thou doeseth, thou shalt faceth the hereafter in a vortex of puree purgatory – the shitteth kind from a jareth.

Of course, there are many sensible and informative responses in the same forums about BLW to offset the lunacy. And yes, this being the internet, there was plenty of belligerent counter attack from the 'traditional' camp, including 'get the stick out of your arse', 'you sound as boring as your food' and, my personal favourite, 'don't be so f***ing puree-tanical' (I can forgive a little aggression for some decent word play).

To be clear, I have friends who baby-led weaned their children (and did so without 'sticks up their arses'). I also have friends who weaned their kids the 'traditional' route, pureeing, mashing and chopping as they progressed (so were far from 'lazy'). I, for the record, gave both finger food as well as spoon-fed puree (very often care of Heinz, Cow & Gate and Ella's Kitchen) to Zain and Yasmin. We were all just feeding our children the best way we saw fit, while minding our own. So this world of dogmatic, overinflated, hypercritical opinion about how a child is provided with sustenance and is taught to eat is just a load of bollocks, surely? The train journey is different, but we all arrive at the same destination. So why the aggressive sanctimony around one particular method over another? And what's all the puree shaming about?

I just don't get it, because…

[Touches earpiece]

[Shuffles papers]

… this news just in:

KIDS WILL NOT GROW UP TO BE NOBEL-PRIZE WINNERS BECAUSE OF HOW THEY WERE FED AS FUCKING BABIES!

I was so excited about weaning both Zain and Yasmin because I truly believe food *is* love. In my experience, you can't have a parent of South Asian descent and not know this. It's in every pinch of perfect seasoning. It's in a perfectly blended, overnight marinade that completely transforms a dish. It's in the hours of stirring, simmering and nurturing a sauce. I have friends of Greek, Italian, Portuguese, Middle Eastern, North African and Turkish heritage who all share similar stories of watching their parents cook the food of their homelands with the same care and devotion. Like me, they too recounted the generous happiness that would radiate from their parents as they tended to the appetites of the people they loved most with vast amounts of food.

'Are you hungry?' Papa will sing moments after you walk through his front door. 'Eat, Pete!' he'll order, even though Pete has already protested three times he's stuffed to capacity with an immense meal Papa has prepared. 'Come, my baby, Papa give you white chocolate mice,' he'll soothe at either Zain or Yasmin (usually after one of them has had a telling-off from me that Papa wants to both make amends for and show his disapproval of). Papa, like many parents of South Asian backgrounds, true to stereotype, has always shown love with food. Even in our days of regularly dining on frozen ready meals, he would ask us repeatedly if we'd eaten enough, often reaching for the milk of magnesia if the amount of food left on our plates warranted concerns for an upset tummy.

So for the 'Papa portion' of this chapter as has clearly become my form, I'd like to walk you through the rules of doing food true to my roots…

How to do food like a parent of South Asian descent

Rule 1: A person cannot possibly know if they're hungry until they've heard all there is to eat in the house

'What can I make for you? Shall I put a couple of samosas in for you? I got French stick – you want French stick? With some cheese? Do you want biscuits? Chocolate? I have seven tubs of the ice cream you like. Why you not eating, Zee? You not well?'

The words 'I'm not hungry' will never register with my dad. You might as well be uttering those words into a black void of space. As he reels off every single edible item he has in the house, I'll try hard to keep from reverting to my teen self when Papa would insist to every friend I brought home that they had to eat *something* the minute they crossed the threshold.

'They said they're not hungry!' I'd eventually snap around the point Papa was listing the seventy-eighth item of food he had to offer and had begun emptying the contents of his fridge. But still Papa would insist they had to eat.

There's a scene in the film *My Big Fat Greek Wedding* you might have seen. It's when Toula's mum, Maria, asks Toula's new boyfriend, Ian Miller, if he's hungry, and when he says he's already eaten, Maria replies, 'OK, I'll make you something.' I very much relate to this scene.

I'll never forget my lovely friends Carla and Sarah, when we were about eighteen, sweetly shushing me for chastising Papa when he'd presented a table practically buckling under the weight of freshly made curry, after stoutly refusing to accept they'd already had their dinners. As I watched them politely and heroically dining on the feast before them, all the while complimenting Papa on his cooking, I knew these were friends for life. Anyone who shows that much understanding for your dad's need to feed are the sort of people you want in your life. These people are my Ian Miller.

Rule 2: Ask your child daily what they have eaten throughout the day. Ask them regardless of age

I rang my dad every day while I was living in London, and each time I'd get the same question at some point during the conversation: 'What you ate today, Zee?' It drove me mad. I'd impatiently give him an overview of that day's diet and then he'd further enrage me with a question like: 'From where you got the sandwich?'

My exasperation would escalate, and I'd snap: 'Jeez, why do you need know where I got the sandwich from?'

'Because I like to know these things,' Papa would protest. 'I like to know what my daughter's eating.'

I now totally get it.

'You've already asked me what I ate at school!' Zain will complain when I've forgotten what his answer was.

'But I need to know what you're eating!' I'll gripe, much like Papa, as I check in his rucksack with the diligence of a forensic scientist to make sure his snack and bottle of water were both consumed. And NOTHING broke my heart more than when he hadn't told me he was required to bring his own daily piece of fruit to school, and I discovered his adorable friend Archie had been sharing his dried mango pieces with him. Images of Zain holding out his hands like Oliver Twist haunted my dreams for weeks… [breaks down into shoulder-shuddering sobs].

*Rule 3: Do not adhere to any health and
safety when cooking*

Being around a relative of South Asian descent while they
are cooking is not for the faint-hearted. Searing hot oil spits
angrily from the hob, with fat raining all around them, as they
indifferently fry meat or batches of furiously popping paneer. A
threadbare tea towel is used as an oven glove to pull out blistering
baking trays of naan and pakora. Scalding items are removed
from the microwave bare-handed with the ease of extracting a
milk bottle from a fridge. And of course, expiration dates are for
namby-pamby losers.

'Those dates are just a guide,' Papa often retorts, retrieving
whatever latest rusty can of food is being brandished accusingly at
him. Try as I may to venture that five years out of date is perhaps a
bit excessive, I know that the can will not be leaving the cupboard
any time soon. Because, you can trust, when the apocalypse strikes,
Papa will be smugly dining on those tins of soup and yam leaves,
and I will be hungrily eating my words.

*Rule 4: Remind your child A LOT that all Indian restaurant
food can be cooked (much better) and consumed in
the comfort of your home*

To go to an Indian restaurant or order a curry is often like a knife to
the heart for South Asian parents. Lines of defence about enjoying
a meal with no washing-up, or treating yourself to a night out,
are wasted breath. It all boils down to this simple fact: why would
you spend money on inferior food?

I don't often voluntarily tell Papa that we've had an Indian
takeaway. I know that he'll first ask (yes, you guessed it) if I've won
the lottery and then sound a little injured that we didn't eat the
lovely curry his freezer is bursting with. I tried explaining once that

Yasmin is currently obsessed with chicken tikka masala (which, as any self-respecting person of South Asian heritage knows, is just throwing a sugary orange sauce on a bed of rice). So Papa, being the kind soul he is, put aside his own antipathy towards the insult to Indian cuisine and attempted to make chicken tikka masala for his granddaughter. Of course, it was far too good to resemble anything as sweet and sickly as the original, and Yasmin ended up just nibbling as little as possible, very clearly just killing time until the ice-cream afters. In fact, Papa would have been better off spooning the ice cream directly onto some basmati and handing it to her, given it's pretty much the same recipe.

Rule 5: Margarine is basically spread that comes with free Tupperware

When I reach for the Clover or Anchor spreadable from Papa's fridge, as I'm about to butter the bread for the kids' sandwiches, I will often stop mid knife plunge and realise I'm about to dip into partially defrosted dahl. It can be a little disorienting and a bit like entering Mr Topsy Turvy's world.

Similarly, one should not get their hopes up around an old biscuit or Quality Street tin, because the chances are the disappointing contents will be several hundred packets of spices or, more randomly as I discovered recently, a gazillion clear plastic bags (the kind you get on a roll at the supermarket near the fruit and veg). These bags, along with the many wire twists saved from the days when sliced bread was sealed with such devices (roughly twenty years ago), will keep things like open packets of biscuits and cheese fresh for longer. And I can chuckle all I like about the many Clover tubs, wire ties and plastic bags Papa hoards, because, again, come the apocalypse, I'll be laughing on the other side of my malnourished face.

Rule 6: Anyone attending a South Asian wedding will require a hearty appetite and an outfit with a lot of 'give'

The biryani at the many Indian-Muslim weddings I've attended is second to none. When I was a kid visiting South Africa, massive vats of it greeted the guests, often hundreds of us, filing in for the walima (the reception). Behind each was a cook stirring and sometimes chucking in massive, last-minute handfuls of seasoning. The smell of the meat, rice, cinnamon, cumin and coriander was something I wanted to bottle and sniff on sad days.

Before tucking into the mutton biryani (seriously, mutton in a wedding biryani is not like any mutton you might have tasted before), a bowl of gajar halwa was presented on each table for guests to help themselves to. Gajar, a very ghee-rich carrot and condensed milk dish, was a starter as per Sunni Gujarati-Muslim tradition (in many other cultures it's given as a pudding due to its sweet nature). Between the biryani I always had seconds of, the dessert (something like semolina drenched in almondy, cardamom-infused cream) and the gajar which I love, it's probably a good thing I don't attend as many South African-Indian weddings these days because I'd be tipping over into Type 2 for sure.

Many more modern Muslim weddings are often slightly less traditional now, with waiter service and a more Western style of presentation. But the principle is the same: arrive hungry, opt for loose-fitting clothing and put aside any concerns for your arteries.

Rule 8: 'Plain tea' is NOT an option

Among my older South African family, a cup of tea is not complete without a biscuit, piece of toast topped with jam, halwa or confectionary of some description.

One afternoon during a visit to South Africa in my early twenties, one of my aunties asked me if I wanted tea, and as I accepted the cup and saucer handed to me, I politely declined the proffered plate of buttered Marie Biscuits.

'What? No Marie Biscuit with your tea?' My auntie looked confused.

'I'm good with just the tea, thanks, Auntie,' I replied, sensing her disorientation as I sipped.

'Plain tea?' She frowned in disbelief. 'Just plain tea?'

In walked my cousin to the kitchen. 'You know, Zeena just wants plain tea?' my auntie said, turning in her seat to fully address her daughter with her staggered face.

My cousin stopped mid pouring from the teapot. 'Plain tea?' she repeated, looking at me.

'That's what I said!' my auntie's voice was booming. 'Plain tea!'

'You don't want a Marie Biscuit with that tea?' asked my cousin, looking concerned.

'I'm not really hung—' I began before stopping myself. I looked at both their perplexed faces, their big, brown eyes wide with incomprehension, almost pleading with me to make sense of this 'plain tea' nonsense. Sometimes you've just got to put your own needs aside and do what's right for your family. 'Actually,' I said breezily. 'Maybe I will have a Marie Biscuit.'

The relief in the kitchen was tangible.

I stumbled across a South African shop in Bristol a while ago and when I spotted the Marie Biscuits, I felt the urge to both laugh and cry. I could smell my auntie's kitchen, fragrant with the day's cooking. I could feel the warm, guava-laced breeze drifting through the open kitchen door. I could picture the confounded, curious faces of my auntie and cousin. I could feel the yearning I had to be sitting in that kitchen drowning in my South African family's love.

I love how emotional food, however simple, can make you. For me, that's exactly the relationship I want my kids to have with food. I want them to feel the warm context of generations of family around it. I want them to eat or smell a certain food and equate happy memories with it. I want them to relish eating the way my family has always savoured it. This, for me, is the healthiest and most important part of my children's relationship with food – not how they learned to chew!

Like Papa, I will always ask them what they ate that day and greet them the second they're through the front door with an itemised account of every bit of food I have in the house. I will check their foreheads for temperatures when they say they're not hungry. And yes, I will probably ignore their friends' pleas that they've already eaten and present plates of food they feel obliged to consume. Because I'm a Moolla. And food is love.

CHAPTER TEN

Working like a Motherfucker

*'You know, Zeena, women have always
had it much harder at work'.*

So, I'm going to put a little extra graft into this chapter at being the mum mate I promised to be at the start of the book. I want to offer some reassurance in case you're planning on returning to work after maternity leave and are feeling in any way daunted by it. But I'm also going to be honest with you. As ever. Because, remember, as Gloria Steinem said, the truth will set you free – but first it might piss you off a bit…

Let's start with some of that cut-to-the-chase candour I'm partial to: I was shitting it about returning to work after having Zain. As much as I thoroughly loved my job as an editor, and the really lovely people I worked with, I was not looking forward to going back at all. I sobbed on Pete as the return date loomed: 'What if I can't do my job anymore? How can I be expected to hand my baby over to a stranger as if the past nine months just haven't happened? What if they don't look after him properly? What if they try to get hold of me for an emergency and I'm in a meeting? What if other babies are mean to him?'

Once back in the office, I then proceeded to cry (the really ugly, blotchy kind), randomly throughout the day, as my friend, colleague and fellow mum Michelle very gently suggested that perhaps the framed picture of Zain practically obscuring my Mac wasn't helping matters.

She was right of course. I took the photograph home and by the end of the week, while I was still wobbly admittedly, I felt a lot stronger for it. (It was an insanely cute photo; the type with the front two teeth on their bottom gums poking through, so they look like cartoon babies and wipe your memory completely clean of the excruciating nights lost to those adorable gnashers.)

After a couple of weeks, Zain and I both settled down. Zain was really happy, and I stopped phoning his kind, and very patient, nursery almost daily, my voice breaking throughout each call like a prepubescent boy. Soon, I was walking to work, often in an outfit alluding to someone with a job, looking forward to the large latte I always stopped for en route and the trip to Zara in my lunch break.

However, on my second maternity leave with my return date to work imminent, I found myself bricking it again. Leaving one baby was hard enough. Being parted from two babies I feared would tip me into absurd levels of hysteria…

Five excellent reasons why every office needs more working mums!

You can spot a woman back from maternity leave a mile off. She'll be the one with bleary, tear-streaked eyes, clutching and sentimentally sniffing a crusty muslin she'd forgotten about in her deep-pocketed, middle-aged coat. But before you give her a wide berth (no sad dad jokes please), for fear she'll brandish pictures of her kids like a slightly aggressive *Big Issue* seller, this woman should be respected. Don't let the misjudged, mumsy M&S back-to-work outfit fool you – she has more skill than Alan Sugar can shake a shaming 'you're fired' finger at. Here are five EXCELLENT reasons why every office needs more working mums…

1. She is fucking productive

Let's start with the biggie, shall we? So big we need an expletive to get the point across. When you've breastfed a baby while simultaneously paying a bill, cleaning every available surface with a wet wipe and spooning Cheerios into a toddler's mouth, you know a thing or two about multi-tasking. A mother of a young baby can make every minute count – because she has to. Essentially, her boss while on maternity leave has been a very unsympathetic tyrant who hasn't allowed her a lunch, tea or toilet break even. Showers, shits and online shopping were squeezed into precious minutes while her baby was strapped into a high chair like Hannibal Lecter, with a rice cake jammed in his mouth.

It's true, instead of a meeting agenda she might absent-mindedly hand over a sticky consent form intended for the childminder's trip to the city farm, and OK, you might lose ten minutes of that conference as she shares the joyous news that little Amy did her first poo on the 'big potty' – but the woman is impressive. Run ragged between her home and work life, and still smiling like a loon because she's taught another human being to excrete into a lavatory? Now *that* is dedication to a (big) job.

*2. She can bring a lovely homely feel to
a basic Formica desk*

Aside from the obligatory framed picture of her kids, a working mum is likely to have a comedy *Is It Friday Yet?* mug, sitting on a coaster encasing a laminated photo of her kids, adjacent to a mousepad featuring yet another photo of her kids. She'll also have a backrest, footrest, small vase of flowers and selection of snacks in the top tray of her stacked files in case of visiting colleagues. If she could, she'd get John Lewis in to fit a nice set of curtains for the window nearest her desk.

Her workmates might pity her as she reaches for one of the hundred plastic spoons in her top drawer (all nicked from Boots in her lunch hour), and feel sadder still when she fills the spoon with one of the thousand sachets of sugar she's pinched from Greggs, but let's be clear, she does not need sympathy. She's not feathering her work nest to compensate for being there – this is her haven! She'll drink that coffee while it's still hot, without interruption from the ascending red lights of a baby monitor. And later, when you see her whistling happily with a copy of *Look* magazine under her arm, she's off to her own personal Promised Land – the ladies' loos. You might want to give it five minutes before you head in there after her.

3. She can pick her battles and is a good loser

This woman knows defeat. The frustration of unsuccessful pitches and bad sales have nothing on failed attempts to get a child to nap or eat some salad; but thanks to a life without the luxury of time or HR department, a mum learns very quickly the art of regrouping.

When she swayed for forty-five minutes to get her baby to sleep, carefully lowering her into the cot and slowly creeping to the door, she could have kicked off like caged wild cat when the baby then woke screaming, arms outstretched to be picked up. Instead, however (after admittedly hurling a tub of Sudocrem against the wall), she scooped up her child, switched on *This Morning* and let her nap on her withered, weary chest. Similarly, when her overtired, tantrumming toddler screamed incessantly in her face for twenty solid minutes because she had the audacity to present a piece of cucumber on his lunchtime platter, she thumbed a copy of *Grazia* and ate the offending cucumber, before replacing it with some Mini Cheddars.

But don't be fooled – she is no pushover. Oh, this woman is clever. Eventually, much like Malcolm X, she'll adopt the by-any-means-necessary approach and get that non-napping child sleeping, and that cucumber consumed, even if it does involve all kinds of manipulation and bribery – which, if you think about it, is a big part of most business.

4. She has a massive bag packed with EVERYTHING

The office Trendy Twenty-Something is likely to openly scoff when her working mum colleague flurries in every day, flooring people as she bustles by with a bag the size of a Fiat Pinto. She might even grimace slightly as she watches the mammoth monstrosity disembark heavily, collapsing in exhausted relief, onto the floor next to her own Aztec, asymmetric miniscule affair from ASOS – but frankly, Working Mum's bag shits all over Trendy Twenty-Something's. That ugly vast bag is like a Co-op in portable PVC form.

Blister? You'll find a Peppa Pig plaster in the zip-up compartment, top right. Mid-morning hangover munchies? There's a packet of Mini Cheddars in the front pouch with the tatty Velcro closing. Unexpected period? Help yourself to the battered tampon sitting proudly on top of the Lamaze teething toy. This bag knows no bounds. Like its owner, it's a bit awkward, battered and cumbersome but is prepared for every possible situation life might throw at it.

Trendy Twenty-Something shouldn't get her hopes up too much though – that stuff scattered all over the bottom of Working Mum's bag is formula, and not the same white powder she has sitting at the bottom of her Class A clutch bag…

5. She doesn't 'have balls' – she has VAGINA

OK, this is the serious shit. This woman has given birth and no matter how that baby was extracted from her body, the experience, even in the most straightforward of circumstances, will have left her feeling like she'd just gone twenty rounds with Anthony Joshua.

And let's not forget the pregnancy. Nine months of growing a human before an experience that ain't called labour for nothing. Warrants a little recuperation, surely?

But there was no post-operative recovery! She was wheeled out, slung on the maternity ward to immediately get to grips with breast-feeding, before the next labouring woman was trundled in faster than an Aldi checkout. You want an employee with inner strength, determination and endurance skill? HIRE A MOTHER! Because to quote the *wonderful* actress Betty White: 'Why do people say "grow some balls"? Balls are weak and sensitive. If you wanna be tough, grow a vagina. Those things take a pounding.' A-fucking-(wo)men!

I think we need new expressions to replace the ridiculous 'grow some balls' and 'he's got real bollocks' style of sayings.

'We're all gonna need some real vagina for this project!'

'She's a force of foof that woman!'

'He's got a lotta clit clout!'

I'll keep working on it…

Mothers in arms

So (moving on) in the interests of providing some of that positivity I promised, I asked a sample of friends how they felt about returning to work and, particularly, the stuff they relished about it. Each also gives a top tip for kicking mum guilt up the arse, because as many mothers know, it can be a motherfucker if you don't nip it in the bud early. And you really should.

Here's what they said:

Wendy, mother of one, scriptwriter and woman who, while enormously loves her child, also loves her job, which she's fucking awesome at:

'You know that bit in The Shawshank Redemption *where Tim Robbins crawls through the prison sewer and comes out into rain and stands there with his arms outstretched, drinking in the joy of finally being free? Well, that's what I felt like the first time I dropped my daughter at the childminder's. I knew I would miss her to bits, but I was so looking forward to getting back to work because I'd missed that too. And frankly, if I'd had to spend one more day of singing 'Wheels on the Bus' I would've lost the will to live.'*

Wendy's top tip for kicking mum guilt up the arse:

'I saw going back to work as something that would only benefit my daughter in the long run. She has an example of a mother who likes her job and works hard at it for everyone's sake. I think reminding yourself of how your child ultimately gains always helps.'

Pritti, mother of two, teacher of secondary-school kids and, therefore, deserves a freaking medal (and you know, better pay and stuff):

'In all honesty, with my return date looming on my first maternity leave, I can't really say I was relishing being with other people's children all day when I couldn't be with mine. But then soon, I was looking forward to the drive to and from work. It was twenty-five minutes of just "me" time! And in fact, the only time I had by myself all day!'

Pritti's top tip for kicking mum guilt up the arse:

'I went back to work after five months with both my kids! The only way I could get sleep with both was through co-sleeping. It

*worked for me. If it works for you too, and it's all safe, do not let
any dick make you feel embarrassed about that!'*

Anna, mother of two, enormously talented senior content
creator and owner of a very cute handbag I want to borrow:

> *'It was the sensibly-sized handbag that brought me back-to-work
> joy; filled not with raisin-coated nappies, spare trousers, general
> litter, baby bottles, snot-drenched tissues and a tiny plastic bag
> containing wet (or worse) pants. Instead, there is high-end
> stationary! Lipstick! Headphones! Five years on and the novelty
> hasn't completely worn off.'*

Anna's top tip for kicking mum guilt up the arse:

> *'In our house, child-rearing duties are split equally(ish) between
> me and my husband. It's a good example to set for our daughters
> and means I'm not the one always shouldering the parental
> guilt. Because I'm pretty sure I wasn't alone when our kids were
> conceived…'*

Kelly-Marie, mother of one, content editor, highlighting
impeccably the merit of a decent mum mate at work:

> *'Everyone raves about the hot cups of tea, but for me it was the
> conversations we had over them, where fellow working mums
> schooled me in the intricacies of not missing the nativity play and
> negotiating with nursery when you're ten minutes late again. They
> helped me see it was possible. I could do it. They were friendships
> formed in the struggle, and the only way I made it through a
> working day on three hours' sleep and always smelling faintly of
> milky sick.'*

Kelly-Marie's top tip for kicking mum guilt up the arse:

'Don't waste time sweating milestones – especially when you're back at work and have enough on your plate. All kids find their own way in the world. I had a friend who swore blind that her son was hugely gifted and surpassing all expectations, but he still shat under my dining table when they came over. Right on the carpet.'

Sarah, mother of two, retail sales supervisor, coffee lover and actual achiever of the working-mum's dream:

'There were two things I was thinking as I was due to go back to work. First: "I can drink hot coffee whenever I want to!" And second: "I hope to God my baby girl is good for my mum and dad so they don't hand her back saying they cannot cope." (They didn't!) I think I actually preferred my job after children. I worked fewer hours, had less responsibility and I could enjoy both my lives.'

Sarah's top tip for kicking mum guilt up the arse:

'Going back to work gave me and my husband new topics to talk about and gossip to share. It wasn't all baby food, nappies and poo! You start to feel less preoccupied with guilt when you have other things to think about and discuss.'

Charmaine, mother of three, ward administrator in a children's emergency department and rock-solid NHS goddess:

'Returning to work after having my children meant my world view became wider and I was no longer sweating the small things at home. Things also became a little easier at work once I started wearing nipple pads. Because no one tells you (or maybe I didn't

pay attention) that other babies crying will also bring down a fresh milk supply and no colour of clothing will help disguise those circular stains of motherhood that greet people before you do. As I was working in the kids' hospital, those nipple pads came in very useful…'

Charmaine's top tip for kicking mum guilt up the arse:

'Don't put too much pressure on yourself to "do it all". Just prioritise the really important stuff, and don't be scared to cut corners. Trust me, the whole family benefits from cutting a few corners.'

Nkiru, mother of two, far from an idiot (actually, very, very clever), summing up perfectly how working mums are often fucked over before they can even consider a job:

'To be honest I hated my job, but I did often fantasise about going back to work, just to spend a few hours in a room that didn't contain my kids. Every mum needs that and work is often the perfect means to remind yourself of your whole identity. However, the childcare costs and the train fare alone would have left me worse off financially, so it didn't make sense. These days, with my kids at school, I'm finding it hard to convince people I'm not an idiot after a decade at home.'

Nkiru's top tip for kicking mum guilt up the arse:

'You have to look after yourself in order to look after your children, so sometimes, let you be the priority. Whether it's lowering your standards or sticking the kids for an afternoon in front of CBeebies so you can have a coffee or just sit in peace for a bit, do it and do it without apology.'

I know, I have very funny and clever friends. I'm quite glad that none of them are writing a humorous non-fiction parenting book, to be frank.

Now, having gone through some of the encouraging aspects a return to work can bring [gear change], I want to address some of that truth that will set you free after it pisses you off a bit. I want to discuss the ridiculous attitudes working mums often have to deal with. And by the way, I know all mums, whether they're at home with their kids or not, are all 'working mothers', but in the absence of any decent alternative shorthand, I've opted for 'working mums' as a well-known term for women who are both mums and have another job outside motherhood. I blame the self-elected internet police for making me this pedantic.

There's a bit in the film *I Don't Know How She Does It* (a very underrated rom com in my opinion) where Christine Hendricks' character points out that if a man announces he's going to leave the office to be with a child, he'll be hailed as a 'selfless, doting, paternal role model'. If a woman, however, has to leave work to be with her sick kid, she'll be damned as 'disorganised, irresponsible and showing insufficient commitment'. My dad, one such man, wholeheartedly agrees.

When I was preparing for my return to work after Zain, he once again blew me away with his inimitable, unfeigned frankness: 'Women have always had it much harder at work, Zee, and once they have children, they have to prove themselves even more,' Papa warned. 'If I couldn't make it into work or had to leave early because one of you was sick, everyone, including women, was far more sympathetic to me than they were to a single mother who had to do the same.

'I saw it a lot in my job – especially when women were coming back from maternity leave. And if they were working part-time hours they were often more or less doing a full-time job – just in less time and for less money! And they were expected to be grateful for this "flexible working"!'

Obviously, it was something I'd already witnessed a lot with friends and colleagues who'd had babies and returned to work, but hearing it from my then 76-year-old dad calling out misogyny in the workplace made me want to squeeze his bristly cheeks with affection. And of course, he was right, like many of my friends could testify as they worked like trojans, preparing presentations while cooking, answering emails as they ran baths and hammering on laptops late into the evening, just so they could keep the different work arrangement they'd been made to feel had been a favour.

My place of work was fortunately pretty supportive and when I eventually moved from full-time to part-time in an attempt to strike the elusive 'work-life balance' that often litters the covers of magazines, my job was both enjoyable and manageable. But that feeling of constantly being on the back foot, especially when your child is sick and you need to be with them, is really unpleasant. Like many mums, I often felt torn between mum and work guilt. Remarks like these did not help:

- *'I tried to find you yesterday afternoon, Zeena, but you weren't in? Was Yasmin ill again?'* [Said by an ambitious, childfree millennial the day after I'd been in hospital with Yasmin because she had bacterial pneumonia.]
- *'What days are you in again, Zeena? You weren't at your desk this morning and I thought today was one of your days in the office.'* [Said by the same ambitious, childfree millennial on a group email, which included my boss, when I'd been tag-teaming with my in-laws, relieving me of looking-after-sick-kid duty – something my boss was thankfully aware of.]

- *'Your child needs to grow some bollocks! He's always sick!'*
  [Said by a colleague about Zain, then eight months old,
  not long after he started nursery and was catching bugs,
  as babies frequently do, virtually back-to-back in the first
  month. Betty White would have made mincemeat of her.]

These comments were the only ones I'd ever really received,
because, as I say, my open-plan office was packed with so many
kind people. But those remarks weren't easy to shake off. They
made me feel like shit. Like many working mums, I worried I
was both failing at home and work, and such asides corroborated
that. And while neither colleague had any sort of real beef with
me (that I'm aware of), the lack of care and empathy was hard
to forgive.

This pitiless attitude was explicitly epitomised in a tweet I
stumbled across, during a week when I had to work from home
for a day because Yasmin, ever a magnet for every germ when she
was very little, was again poorly. (My brilliant boss was amazingly
sympathetic in such matters, by the way; she'd only ever ask after
Yasmin's well-being and always encouraged a no-bullshit, mutual
respect. I know, I was a jammy cow.)

This is what 'Becky' tweeted (her name changed and Twitter
handle omitted, just so it's clear I'm not attempting to send a
baying mob her way): *'Recently, a mum I work closely with has
taken a number of "working-from-home" days to look after a child
with scarlet fever. Meanwhile, I'm left to pick up the pieces. Perhaps
I can invent a fake kid so I can do the same…'*

I'm generally not one for being the instigator of @ing people
on the internet. It rarely ends well, all opinions concerned remain
unchanged and you lose precious time in your life that you'll never
see again. The only people who stand anything to gain are the
social-media lurkers, revelling in the tetchy exchange. So instead,
I drafted an Instagram post in response to that shameful tweet.

This is the unedited version before Instagram's character count rudely forced me to sub it:

Dear Becky,

I saw your tweet regarding your issues around a colleague working from home in order to tend to her child with scarlet fever. I'd like to respond to your tweet if I may…

First, I'd like to say, I was single and 'child free' for MANY years before meeting my other half and having kids. And believe me, I have not forgotten how trivialised your life can feel because of fuckwits who can't make sense of a person not in a relationship, and – horror of horrors – a woman of childbearing age without kids.

I'm old enough to remember the hideously offensive 'single tables' at weddings. If you're unfamiliar, this is where 'unaccompanied' guests, largely female and maybe the occasional gay man, were parked like a sort of miscellany of misfits, usually somewhere near the loos, where we were, I presume, expected to claw like starving peasants for the bouquet.

So, with such bittersweet, life-shaping memories, on the whole, I prefer to give the mum mob quick to lynch a child-free critic a swerve…

HOWEVER, after a week in which my four-year-old has been burning up and hacking like a forty-a-day Lambert & Butler addict, meaning that yes, on one day, I did have to work from home, your tweet really pissed me off.

Becky, any chance of an intelligent point about how society marginalises women without kids is lost thanks to trashing your workmate on Twitter. Your real beef should be with your bosses and the support you clearly feel lacking.

And, Becky, those inverted commas around the words working from home, and suggesting you could invent a fake kid in order to do the same, imply you think she's skiving – and not, if I can speak from my own experience, working twice as hard to ensure she can keep that flexibility in her job.

And, Becky, please believe me when I say 'working mum guilt' is not a myth. It might have been your colleague's choice to have kids (a fairly tedious line bandied frequently by regular working-mum bashers), but surely you can empathise? Maybe you'll make a life choice one day you'd like people to show support and compassion for? Who knows, it might even be something you need some flexibility in your working arrangement to accommodate for.

And, Becky, BECKS! Women in the workforce, with or without kids, have enough shit to deal with. We should have each other's backs. We shouldn't be stabbing them.

I wish you love and joy.

Zeena

The likes of 'Becky' aside, going back to work can be, overall, a very happy experience. And genuinely, despite my initial reticence both times, I genuinely loved it. It's true, working for a decent company helps, but there are things to help you ease back after maternity leave wherever you work, and I want to help if I can.

Brace yourself, I might actually offer something resembling advice here…

Top tips for returning to work and not losing your shit

1. Find the childcare that has your total trust and back

You'll feel infinitely happier once you have the right day care for your kid. The nursery we chose for Zain near Pete's office was a godsend.

When I met his two keyworkers, I liked them immediately. They were kind, genuine and there was no hard sell, just a reassuring sense from them they were there to accommodate us and not the other way around. They were a breath of fresh air, especially having visited other nurseries where requesting a space very much felt like approaching a snooty maître d' at an exclusive restaurant without a reservation. I also thankfully had my incredibly generous mother-in-law, who had offered up two days a week of childcare so I could work full-time. She was like a baby whisperer with both my two and, to this day, she is the one I trust the most with my kids. This is the sort of comfort and assurance a working mum needs in her life.

2. NEVER apologise for being a mum

Life has changed. So what if you're unable to stay late because you have to pick up your baby from childcare on time? Who cares if you can't make a lunchtime trip to the pub because you have to leg it round town to buy nappies and something for dinner? You're a working mum trying to make every second count. You can't be all things to all people, and any decent person gets this.

Remember also, if you're asking for any reasonable flexibility around your working arrangement or empathy for a particular mum-related situation, don't approach the situation like you're requesting a huge favour. You're not asking for an organ donation! And you shouldn't be made to feel as if you are. You can always assess how you feel after the conversation, but in the meantime, be clear, polite, helpful but never apologetic just because you're a mother with specific needs.

3. Find your work-mum tribe

Seek out other working mums, in your office, among your friends or online. Again, it's not because childfree women can't make sense of your life, because after having both my kids, I found my office full of hugely supportive people, lots of them without children. Often, however, like Kelly-Marie mentioned, it helps to have other mothers in your life who 'get' those working-mum-specific issues from first-hand experience. When I needed advice about childcare vouchers, wanted to bluster about an ambitious millennial making me feel crap or just blub because I was missing my kids, having someone who'd been through it all really helped curtail feeling alienated [waves at Michelle].

4. Share the shit at home

My wise friend Anna touched on this in her tip. If you have a partner, you each need to pull your weight! 'The mental load' is not just the creation of a French feminist cartoon. It's in every phone reminder you set to pay a bill or ring the nursery. It's in every list you draw up for shopping or household jobs that need doing. It's in every half-completed chore that you've requested ('You asked me to unload the dishwasher – you didn't say anything about *reloading* the dishwasher.') It's time to divvy up the homelife work! Sure, it might involve some instigation and delegation from you initially (and obviously 'project managing' is still a part of the mental load), but at least you'll be moving away from bearing it all alone. Because, particularly after maternity leave, many women are knackering themselves doing way more than they should. As Anna (sort of) said, it took a foof *and* a willy to make your baby; don't let the willy dick about.

5. Resist quitting while you're in a back-to-work funk

There will be tough days. You might feel that it would be easier to be at home and succumb solely to the pretty gruelling-in-itself job of being a mother. But, particularly in those early weeks after returning, when you convince yourself that the slog is worse than Prisoner Cell Block H and you can all survive on baby porridge if you put your minds to it, don't make any hasty decisions. This is a new job, even if you're returning to the same role, because you're treading a lot of unfamiliar territory that needs adapting to. So consider the first three months a sort of probationary period for both you and your job. Because for most of us, money is a necessity, not a luxury, and while no one should ever be desperately unhappy, it's important to have a clear head before you flip off your boss.

6. Remember, my dad thinks you should know your worth...

'Too many mothers undersell themselves at work, Zee,' said Papa recently when I was discussing this particular chapter with him. 'When I was working in the civil service, I saw so many women after having children working harder than anyone else to make sure there was no excuse for complaint whatsoever. They hit the ground running the minute they sat down and barely looked up until the work was done. Those women were some of the most productive in the office! And yet, you know, Zeena, they didn't know their worth. Because some big show-off man with designer shoes, who didn't have anywhere near as much skill, could get a job over them with just ego and fancy talk. If you put this in the book, Zee, you can make it sound better if you want.'

Nope. I can't. Because Papa nailed it.

I have never had a job like motherhood. I have never worked as hard. I have never been more exhausted. I have never had to adapt so quickly to an ever-evolving role. I have never felt so clueless. I have never experienced so much exasperation. I have never, in my entire life, loved a job so much. I hope you're feeling much the same. And I really hope you know your worth. Because, as ever, Papa is right. You really should.

CHAPTER ELEVEN

When the Shitstorm Blows Over

'You know, reader, I actually quite like this motherhood lark…'

Yasmin: 'Mummy, I've got a joke.'
Me: 'Ooh, I love a joke. Go ahead.'
Yasmin: 'Why did the cat chase the dog?'
Me: 'I don't know, why did the cat chase the dog?'
Yasmin [shrugs]: 'I dunno, what you asking me for?'

She made this up! It's genius, right?

Yasmin told me this joke, which I've since heard approximately 27,000 times, one bedtime as I was tucking her in. She stared at me, poker-faced, with her enormous long-lashed green eyes as I gazed back, slightly frowning with confusion as I digested the joke. Finally getting it, I burst out laughing and squeezed her squidgy cheeks with pride. Yasmin, in turn, gave me a sweet satisfied smile, popped her thumb in her mouth, rolled over onto her side and snuggled into her huge unicorn plush.

I was still chuckling aloud as I snapped on the lamp and noisily exited the room, basking in smugness that at the age of six, my daughter had already nailed deadpan, sophisticated, slightly surreal humour. And it was all her own work! It was a very proud moment for me, and I will, of course, be signing her up for stage school the second she masters the art of nuanced observational comedy and showbiz smiles that don't quite reach the eyes…

The reasons for me sharing this with you are two-fold. One: I like to show off regularly how funny and clever both my children are (they're also kind, generous, loving, ridiculously cute and utterly perfect in every sense, by the way). Two: I couldn't have even begun to imagine a bedtime like this when I first became a mum, while pacing the floor, craving sleep and sanity, holding a baby screaming relentlessly and torturously in my face.

Let me pull out some extra detail for you about that bedtime. Zain was already drifting off in the top bunk. In fact, he'd asked me to tone down my noisy bedtime manner as I was apparently preventing some much-needed, precious sleep (I know, THE NERVE OF IT).

Afterwards, Pete and I flopped on the sofa, a Thai takeaway, good film and very nice bottle of Bordeaux to look forward to. I then retired for a full night of uninterrupted slumber, to dream about unhurried poos in peace and holidays in Tesco's wine aisle.

It might sound as if I'm laying it on a bit thick with the Holy Grail stuff, but I know New-Mum Me hungrily devoured such tales of The Promised Land. The long nights I spent holding Zain upright on my chest so he could kip untroubled by his belly and oesophagus. The evenings I hid at the foot of his cot, face down on the carpet inhaling fluff, waiting for sure signs that REM was occurring before exiting like a silent assassin. The mornings, after returning to work and on the back of a particularly hideous bout of teething when I could have happily smashed my alarm-buzzing phone with a bottle of Calpol. These were all gruelling episodes soothed by stories, as comforting as folklore and proverbs, regaling a world where children slept beautifully and Thai takeaways were eaten at leisure.

I know that it's too easy as a new parent to wish the time away. And honestly? I still have those days. Yasmin's second favourite joke for you:

'Knock, knock!'
'Who's there?'
'Jelly.'
'Jelly, who?'
'Jelly, jelly, jelly!'

I mean, seriously, WTF? Where's the bloody effort? It makes zero sense! And no amount of belly-wobbling on the word 'jelly' will save it! This 'gag' was a favourite for joke-at-bedtime with both Zain and Yasmin for an excruciating amount of time, and each time, as they fell into fits of giggles from their respective bunks, I wanted to rip my ears off so I wouldn't have to listen to that shit knock-knock again.

And there are, of course, other wishing-it-away moments. Nagging them for the eighteenth time to put their shoes on. (Every. Bleeding. Morning.) Doing the walk-of-shame *back* to school with a change of clothes for both kids because I've forgotten a non-school uniform day. The nights when I'm awoken abrasively as Yasmin scrambles over my face, using my eye sockets as footholds, to get into the bed. (Why my husband thought *Jumanji* for our Friday night film was a good idea, I'll never know.) Ask me at any of these points if I'm 'cherishing every moment' and I'll probably moon you my reply.

There will always be new Holy Grails. When they can make their own breakfasts, bathe themselves and go to the offie to buy me wine all feature pretty high on that list. But actually, while it's unlikely you'll find me authoring any zen-like books about mindful parenting any time soon, I can tell you, I find being a mum the dog's bollocks. If you're not there yet, you really will be – and sooner than you think.

While I will never forget the shitstorm of that first year, there are so many happy moments etched in my memory from my new-mum days, and, yin to the yang and all that, I want to share some with you in case you need a little comfort from The Promised Land. And believe me, whittling them down was really hard…

Ten (of approximately ten gazillion) new-mum moments I will cherish forever

1. When Zain first properly recognised me during a late-night feed and kept wrenching on and off the boob to lock eyes and beam at me. I'm sure my nipple was as raw as an uncooked prawn afterwards, but I don't recall that. I only remember the surge of complete and utter undying love that overtook my acute disorientation from having only just fallen asleep.

2. When he'd be so pleased to see me after a lovely long nap (they came eventually), he'd kick his chubby legs and punch his clenched, dimply fists with joy. And don't even get me started on those gorgeous, gummy little smiles… [SOB].

3. When Pete and I would squabble about who'd be the first to retrieve Zain (then 'sleeping through' most nights), from his cot in the mornings, and I'd be genuinely pissed off if Pete beat me to it. The irony of all those nights with us each insisting it was the other's turn to get up was not lost on me.

4. When he first started babbling words around the age of seven months, and as I shopped in Asda, he'd shout from his pram at random, passing, slightly worried-looking men: 'Dada!'

5. When Zain first walked on a pavement by himself and staggered about like the happiest drunk you've ever seen.

6. When Zain fully embraced the contemporary, freestyle dancing he learned at nursery and would prance like a hippy at Woodstock to anything from Pete randomly bashing his toy xylophone to iPhone's default ringtone.

7. When he was almost two and he'd say 'titty' instead of 'pretty'. The memory of him pointing at me and saying 'Mummy's titty' will always both melt my heart and make me wet myself a little.

8. When Zain's love of elephants became apparent, and just the sight of one on the telly would have him squealing with excitement and shouting: 'Eh-phent!' He still sleeps with his stuffed, purple elephant tucked under his arm and, like the massive-hearted boy he is, when he was four, vowed to save all animals from going 'exstink'.

9. When every person who encountered him, with his sweet, thoughtful personality becoming increasingly evident as he progressed through nursery and preschool, used the word 'kind' to describe him.

10. When Zain first said he loved me. I mean, it doesn't get much better than that does it?

Oh, MY! My ovaries are in overdrive just recollecting all this! You see? This is how Mother Nature gets you! She's such a clever cow, that MN…

Those moments still come thick and fast. Every time Yasmin slides onto my lap, reaches for a chunk of my hair and sucks her thumb whenever she's tired or upset, as she has done since she was tiny. Every time Zain relays an animal fact I didn't have a clue about. (Did you know that a koala joey is the size of a jelly bean at birth? Lucky koala mummy, right?) Every time they both give me their 'juiciest' hugs and kisses, each like a shot of serotonin straight to a vein. Every time we finish bedtime with: 'I love you to the moon and back and back again and to infinity and beyond.' These are all deposited in a vault to be opened when they're worrying me sick as teenagers, and leaving home to start lives away from their suffocating mother who never stops asking if they're hungry.

Some people say they want kids. I yearned for a family. And starting a family wasn't at all what I expected. It was insanely hard. But being a family exceeds all expectations, every day. It has, without doubt, made me the happiest I've ever been.

I hope the shitstorm of your baby's first year is passing. I hope you are forming supportive, side-splitting friendships at the coalface of motherhood. I hope your sense of humour is cushioning the shit days. I hope the wealth of everything wonderful there is to look forward to is budding all around you like little auspicious seedlings. I hope you know your baby is lucky to have such a brilliant mum.

CHAPTER TWELVE

Top of the Pops

'You know, Papa, I owe you so much.'

Hello Papa,

I had to close the book addressing you directly. How could I not? This book has meant so much more to me than documenting my experiences of motherhood, against a backdrop of your world-class single-parenting. This book contains your love: your resolute, radiating, life-shaping love that I've been lucky enough to revel in every single day of my existence.

I said in the introduction that I wanted to say something breathtakingly profound to do justice to a human being like you, but nothing felt adequate. Twelve chapters on, and still there are no words that feel in any way satisfactory enough.

Before starting this chapter, I alternated between staring at a blank Word document and deleting every sentence I attempted for an hour, because nothing articulated what you so richly deserved. This is undoubtedly the hardest chapter for me to write. Because there's so much I want to say, and yet so little befitting with which to say it. 'Amazing', 'brilliant', 'wonderful', 'remarkable' – those adjectives sound feeble, almost disrespectful, to come anywhere close to describing a person like you. You deserve your own words. Exclusive, beautiful, poignant words. A whole dictionary filled with them. For the world to reference when looking for definitions of indescribable love.

As I wrote this book and relived some of those memories, I could feel all the warmth you exude when you're not even in the room.

'What a legend!'
'Oh my God, I want to meet your dad!'
'I want your dad to adopt me!'
'He sounds *incredible*!'

These are all the things people have said, when I've relayed an anecdote or memory about you; your humour and kindness flooring them.

You never cease to floor me.

'I'm not Germaine Greer, Zee!' you joked when we were chatting about the inequalities women, particularly mothers, face in the workforce and I'd asked if you'd consider yourself a feminist. And yet in the next breath, you told me about the single-dad support group you joined and promptly left, because 'the misogyny was so disgraceful'.

Chief Albert Luthuli, South African Nobel Peace Prize winner and ANC leader was one of many who waved you off as you left for the UK in your twenties. When you told me about that recently, I couldn't believe I'd gone forty-seven years without knowing this! But then, I shouldn't be surprised, really. Of course he did! It's completely right that a South African hero would have so much affection and respect for another South African hero.

'You must always challenge apartheid, racism, injustice – all of it – wherever you see it, Zee,' you've said to me repeatedly throughout my life. I promise faithfully to do just that. I promise faithfully to teach my kids to do just that.

When I was trying to form heartfelt sentences worthy of you, I ended up drafting an abstract list of things I wanted to thank you for. And despite its random nature, I want to share it in an attempt, at the very least, to express my gratitude. Because I owe you so much, Papa.

Thank you for cooking.

Thank you for cleaning.

Thank you for washing my clothes.

Thank you for ironing my clothes.

Thank you for the nights you hugged a bad dream away.

Thank you for making my world feel safe when it wasn't always.

Thank you for turning sad days around.

Thank you for the fourteen-hour-round-trip car journeys while I was at university.

Thank you for the pixie boots.

Thank you for telling me repeatedly that I should know my worth.

Thank you for supporting me when I said I wanted to be a journalist.

Thank you for openly scoffing when an auntie said I should be a doctor, lawyer – pharmacist at a push – but never a journalist.

Thank you for teaching me the importance of being confident in my voice, however lone.

Thank you for letting me commit some of your wonderful catchphrases to a book.

Thank you for allowing me this with characteristic humour ('Fine, make me sound silly! But then I get half of your profits?').

Thank you for letting me take off your accent.

Thank you for being funny.

Thank you for making me laugh when I really didn't want to.

Thank you for showing me how to harness the therapeutic powers of humour.

Thank you for loving me as a perpetually mortified, sulky teenager.

Thank you for loving me as a perpetually mortified, sulky 47-year-old.

Thank you for loving me unconditionally, dear Papa.

Thank you for being such a selfless parent. My heart aches with fondness recollecting everything you did and sacrificed for your three children.

If I could, along with that dictionary of magnificent words created solely for you, I would write multiple, cumbersome tomes of thank yous. Because that list is not nearly extensive enough. And that list is not nearly comprehensive enough. It doesn't depict the young Indian-Muslim man who travelled thousands of miles from his South African home and founded a life in the UK, worlds apart from the one he left behind. That list does not articulate the hard lump that forms in my throat, just thinking about how much that man surmounted to raise three children alone, wholeheartedly, in a culture so vastly different from his own. That list will always be insufficient, because I cannot thank you enough, Papa.

We've weathered a lot. Life could be harsh, sad at times, but I cannot even begin to express how fortunate I feel to inhabit a world with you as my darling dad. You have given me the kind of parental love that is boundless. The kind of love that shelters you. The kind of love that helps you heal. The kind of love that makes you strong. The kind of love that never asks for anything in return. The kind of love where its presence is felt daily. This is Papa Love. And its legacy will live on.

I love you 599, Papa.
Zee

A LETTER FROM ZEENA

I have one last lot of colossal thanks to make – to you.

However you came across this book, I am thoroughly grateful to you for taking the time to read something that has meant so much to me. If you did enjoy my book and want to keep up with the latest news from me, you can sign up here:

www.thread-books.com/zeena-moolla

(Your email will never be shared, and you can unsubscribe at any time).

I wanted this book to speak to the new mum who perhaps feels her identity isn't always reflected in the media and online world. I hoped to reach the new mum who, standing in front of the parenting-humour shelves of bookshops, doesn't feel her relationship with motherhood is represented here either. I wanted to be a mum mate for that mother feeling alienated. The mother who, as I did, perhaps feels as if she's joined a club she doesn't quite belong to.

Also, very significantly, funny parenting books in the UK often don't reflect any diversity of family life beyond nuclear white British. So when the publisher at Thread, Claire Bord, with a mixed-heritage family of her own, helped mould this book with my father as a backdrop, it felt like the perfect fit. As I said in my introduction, who better to exemplify that loving, healthy families exist in a multitude of ways than Papa?

However, as I also mentioned in my intro, I'm a little over seeing books with any reflection of diversity sitting away from the mainstream, collecting dust in melancholic, fusty-looking jackets. So if you have enjoyed *Everything I've Learned About Motherhood* (and I really hope you have), I would be most grateful if you could take the time to leave a lovely review. Your support would mean an awful lot to both me and Papa, especially as dust tends to aggravate our hereditary eczema.

Thank you SO much.

Lastly, if you'd like to follow Word to the Mothers you can do so below.

I'd love to hear from you (unless you're a troll, and in which case, not so much).

Thank you again. May your life be filled with poos in peace and solo trips to Tesco.

Zeena

 wordtothemothers

 @bristolgirl1973

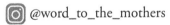 @word_to_the_mothers

ACKNOWLEDGMENTS

Gah! Where do you start with these things? I mean, *obviously* I have practised a lot of acceptance speeches in the shower, largely entailing gasping dramatically, holding aloft a bottle of anti-nit shampoo and hastily doing peace signs, hip-hop style, to the kids' bath toys as some shit kicks off the other side of the bathroom door. But my shower-time efforts have not been sufficient rehearsal for the thanks I owe. And while I don't want to get all Gwynnie P on your arse, I do have a large list of people I wish to express quite a lot of gushy gratitude for. (So, please, don't play the music just yet...)

Firstly, I have to say an enormous thank you to my agent Abi Fellows for her kindness, honesty, humour, rock-solid support and promises of red wine on completion of the book. (I'll have a large Malbec please. And I DON'T want no non-alcoholic nonsense.) I've said it before, and I'll keep saying it: I'm very chuffed you're my agent. You are a total gem, dear Abi.

I also want to thank Nikesh Shukla and Team TGLA for taking a chance on a sweary, sarky mum of two, and also bucking the recurrent publishing prerequisite of a mega-mammoth internet presence that almost had me throwing in the towel. You deserve so much recognition for all the work you do.

Jo Carnegie, you are worthy of all the Sauvignon for encouraging me to get off my sofa-loving backside and write a book in the first place. Thank you for all the feedback and reassurance, you magnificent woman.

Claire Bord; blimey, you are owed a big fat vat of gratitude. I know, thanks to the shitshow of 2020, we are yet to actually meet, but with your wit, good heart and huge talent, you are right up my street. I feel like this book could have only been edited and published by you and the team at Thread. THANK YOU for shaping this book with real soul. It's like you do it for a living or something? Trust me, when we do meet, I'm going to embrace you for a little longer than is comfortable.

Bob Bewick, there is a pie and a pint with your name on for all your amazing creative help. And what the hell, I'll throw in a bag of Lidl crisps too.

Thanks to those frigging AWESOME, sanity-saving mum mates of both maternity leaves: Louisa, Carolyn, Cee, Kate H, Annalise, Simone and Holly.

Thanks to those far-too-funny-for-my-liking friends who contributed quotes for this book: Helen E, Lucy, Helen F, Nikki, Wendy, Pritti, Anna, Kelly-Marie, Sarah P, Charmaine and Nkiru.

MASSIVE love and thanks to those of you on the internet who have engaged so hilariously and supportively with Word to the Mothers. If I could, I'd buy you all a drink (particularly those of you who took the time to call out the joke thieves and take on the anti-vaxxers – you'd get extra-large drinks and maybe a packet of cheese and onion each too).

Thanks to my in-laws, for being so amazing, particularly during those dire acid-reflux days. Sandy, I'll never forget your kindness and I'll do whatever I can to sort that national bank holiday in your honour.

Thank you to Zubie, Fahmeeda and Mohammed for helping me with the written Gujarati of our dialect. *Thane bow pyaar karoonch.*

Thanks to my brother and sister and all my family, present and past, immediate and extended, who make me proud to be a Moolla. How lucky am I to belong to such a warm, loving, generous, HILARIOUS clan of people? And to my South African family specifically, I miss you so much, but one day soon, we'll be reunited in Stanger, feasting on biriyani, sipping Fanta Grape, with Uncle Ismail's phenomenal sense of humour heartening us all like only he can.

Pete, I know I devoted a whole chapter to you, but I'd like to thank you for asking me out in the Big Chill bar that December night in 2009. My life has been so happy since with you in it. And you've been utterly AMAZING while I've been writing this book. I know home-schooling solo during the summer lockdown of 2020 was a stinking pile of pandemic pants, so I think comparing you favourably to other do-nothing dads in this instance is entirely justified. I love you with my whole heart and you still make me a bit funny in my tummy.

And of course, there are two small, but hugely significant, people who I want to devote extra special thanks to: my Zain and my Yasmin. You are both my absolute everything. You make each and every day a total joy. You have brought so much happiness into my life that I cannot even begin to express how much I love you. And if you each decide to have families of your own one day, I want to be there for you, witticism and wine at the ready, but most of all with frequent reminders of how completely worthwhile you both made those difficult days. I love you more than elephants and Princess Jasmine. And you know how much I love elephants and Princess Jasmine.

So I think that's everyone, right? Oh, wait. I think there is someone else? Oh yes! I think there's a bloke called something like Peppy? Or is it Popo? Pippi…?

PAPA! I know I've said it all, but here it is, one last time: THANK YOU. You're not just a wonderful example of loving parenting. You're the embodiment of an exceptional, beautiful human being.

Lightning Source UK Ltd.
Milton Keynes UK
UKHW011841040221
378271UK00001B/97